Fahrenheit 9-12

Also by Aaron I. Reichel, Esq. (partial listing):

Government Disclosure Service, Prentice-Hall, 1979–1983 (Founding Editor)

Style & Usage Manual (Co-Author), Prentice-Hall, 1985

The Maverick Rabbi (Author)
(1st & 2nd editions hardcopy, 1984, 1986, ISBN 0-89865-174-3)
(1st & 2nd editions paperback, 1984, 1986, ISBN 0-89865-299-5)

The Jewish Directory and Almanac, 1986–1988 (Contributor)

Monograph and numerous articles including:
    "Analyzing the FOIA 'Improvements,': Not as Antidisclosure as They May Seem," *The National Law Journal*, Dec. 14, 1981, reproduced by U.S. Senate Committee on the Judiciary's Subcommittee on the Constitution, October, 1982.
    "Perspective: Further Jury Reform Proposals," *New York Law Journal*, July 1, 1994, p. 2.
    "Forum—Stop Perjury by Allowing (sic, should have been by Compelling) Witnesses to Swear on Their Personal Beliefs," *L.A. Daily J.*, Feb. 16, 1999, p. 6.
    "On Equal Rights and the Wage Gap" (putting both in perspective), The Daily Record (serving the legal and business communities of Baltimore), May 9, 1983, follow-up rebuttal June 2, 1983.

Fahrenheit 9-12

Rebuttal to *Fahrenheit 9/11*

Not Quite *FahrenHEIL 9/11*

In Opposition to *FahrenHEIT 9/11*

And in Support of *FahrenHYPE 9/11*

Aaron I. Reichel, Esq.

iUniverse, Inc.

New York   Lincoln   Shanghai

Fahrenheit 9-12
Rebuttal to Fahrenheit 9/11

iUniverse books may be ordered through booksellers or by contacting:

iUniverse
2021 Pine Lake Road, Suite 100
Lincoln, NE 68512
www.iuniverse.com
1-800-Authors (1-800-288-4677)

2nd Edition, 2005

ISBN: 0-595-33740-6 (Pbk)
ISBN: 0-595-67000-8 (Cloth)

Printed in the United States of America

Dedicated to people of all faiths and beliefs—including but not limited to Muslims, Christians, Jews, Buddhists, Hindus, atheists, and agnostics—to the extent they have acted fairly, decisively and kindly on behalf of their fellow human beings in ways that are pleasing to all people of good will.

Contents

About this Book

All people whose lives will continue to be affected directly or indirectly by decisions to be made by the duly elected leader of the free world owe it to themselves, their country, and the rest of their fellow human beings, to at least become aware of who was or was not duly elected in the American presidential election at the beginning of this century, which brought us to the position in which we now find ourselves, and to be knowledgeable about both sides of every other issue raised in the superficially super-persuasive "documentary" known as *Fahrenheit 9/11*.

Although this book is a comprehensive response and rebuttal to the uniquely influential movie known as *Fahrenheit 9/11*, its status in the literature has changed since it was first written. It may no longer necessarily be the most thorough presentation known to the writer—at least three Internet sites cited in this text may vie for this title. It may not necessarily be the most intriguing—the movie and DVDs cited in the text may vie for this title. But it may be the most— or one of the most—well-documented response(s) and rebuttal(s) to have been first published in book form prior to the election of 2004, and just as do the other responses and rebuttals referred to above, it attempts to present some original thoughts and research, and then supplement this material with references to the findings of most of the other compilers of information known to them, giving credit where credit is due. In the event that any omissions of credits will have occurred, we apologize and pledge to fill them in should any future edition(s) of this book be published, if we will be notified in writing and in time. In the event that any errors will have been made, we apologize to our readers and to any aggrieved person(s) or organization(s), and pledge to correct them, if notified of them, should any future edition(s) of this book be published.

The author of this compilation of information recognizes the fairness appropriate in giving Michael Moore some slack, and asks for the same understanding. He cannot possibly vouch for the accuracy of every statement he makes or cites, and cannot be expected to single-handedly search through Iraq for weapons of mass destruction to verify the various findings or lack of findings, nor every other cited statement which may not be quite as difficult or impossible to verify, and hereby makes every statement in the book subject to the accuracy of the cited sources.

This book attempts to be a reader-friendly and moderately thorough resource, responding objectively—but not obsessively—to virtually every argument, insult, punch line, and cinematic device in the movie. The author does not question Michael Moore's integrity or good-faith beliefs, but believes that in Mr. Moore's zeal to undermine the official position of the United States, on various issues, such as the 2000 election and the decision to authorize the 2003 War in Iraq, he may have taken some facts out of context, and in some instances, it seems to many, out of thin air. Furthermore, the author believes that in some cases facts can be brought forth to support two opposing sides of an issue. What you are about to read summarizes some of Mr. Moore's points, as points of reference, and then presents facts and analysis that may lead to very different conclusions.

In lieu of ordinary illustrations or of copied and/or hackneyed caricatures, this book features what we will refer to as *"virtual illustrations,"* in the belief that they are specific enough to create well-focused images in the imaginative minds of virtually all of the readers of this book, on virtually each of the topics discussed in this book, but not so creative as to cause readers to conjure up images that may be false, misleading, and/or otherwise unjustified, no matter what they may have thought upon seeing *Fahrenheit 9/11.*

Unlike most—if not all—of the works on this topic that have already appeared as this book went to press—primarily on the Internet and in periodicals—this one contains an alphabetical list of sources at the end, and an index, as well as, as described above, a "virtual illustration" to accompany virtually each point.

We hereby apologize, in advance, for any errors that may appear in this book, any and all of which, if they exist, are surely inadvertent. We assure you that every attempt will be made to correct any possible errors in future editions (to the extent future editions will be issued, and to the extent notification will be timely). At the same time, we also hope that Mr. Moore will read—or arrange for the reading, on his behalf, of all constructive criticisms of his film, which this work is intended to be—and will apologize promptly, and with specificity, for every error and/or misleading and/or disrespectful statement and cinematic device he will concede having made, to the extent he hasn't done so by the time this book will have been published and distributed.

Virtual illustration of the author or anyone else playing tennis and hitting back a few balls at the same time.

Alternate virtual illustration of two people debating, with an audience of people who look intelligent, while, in another room, some spaced-out dummy-types stare at a bank of televisions with Homer Simpson in each screen.

About the Title

It would be a natural reaction for virtually anyone who sees Michael Moore's spliced footage of President Bush on 9/11 out of context and in a vacuum to come away thinking less of President Bush, and thinking more of Moore. Only after checking out the facts, which became available to most people when they read the newspapers the day after—on 9/12—and later, can one begin to see this scene and all of the other scenes in the movie in perspective. Hence, the title of this book. This book does not take sides as to whether President Bush deserved a second term. It does suggest, however, that anyone exposed directly or indirectly to the film should take a second look at the facts, and see what has been uncovered about virtually every allegation, beginning the day after, and continuing, in print, on the Internet, on DVDs, and in a movie. Dick Morris, one of the principals of the Moore-rebutting DVD *Fahrenhype 9/11*, observed that if you have swallowed the poison of *Fahrenheit 9/11*, the antidote is *Fahrenhype 9/11*. To elaborate on this imagery, we might respectfully point out that if *Fahrenheit 9/11* was more like an epidemic of distortions of epic proportions, raging out of control like a forest fire, and causing the blood of every seeker of the truth to reach the boiling point, then various remedies and medications are needed. At first, many movie reviews were written. By now, some Internet sites go into incredible detail, in spelling out the distortions in the film, and in providing extensive historical and political background. It is inevitable that eventually at least a few different books will be written and published, if they haven't already been by the time this book will be published, identifying and then correcting the apparent distortions. We believe that each presentation serves a purpose. Different people will prefer different media, and different people write with different styles and different degrees of depth. Some readers will not be satisfied until they will have read massive doses of information, and some will be satisfied with a small book review. No small book review, however, no matter how well written, can begin to do justice to correcting the injustices that we believe most people will find in *Fahrenheit 9/11* and in the dearth of publicity regarding the attempts to put it into proper perspective.

There was a temptation to call this book *FahrenHEIL 9/11*, in order to highlight the point that the film *Fahrenheit 9/11* may be viewed as taking propaganda to a height—or should we say a depth—rarely achieved in the Western world of democracies. However, a decision was made <u>not</u> to entitle this book in an inflammatory way for a variety of reasons:

- To make it clear that although we believe that an argument can be made that the film may be viewed as more of a propaganda piece than a documentary, we do NOT believe that it quite stoops to the level of the people who said "heil" to their chief, notwithstanding how offensive we find those who say or said "to hell" with *theirs*;

- We believe it is *possible* that Michael Moore loves democracy, the United States of America, the presidency, and all that is good and nice in the world, notwithstanding his unusual methods of expressing himself in these and other areas;

- However, we also believe that any discussion about leadership—or about any other subject—should be based not only on facts, but also on presenting them fairly, responsibly, respectfully, and in context, and for this reason we wrote this book.

- We wish to make it clear, up front, that we are not accusing Michael Moore of intentionally misleading the American people, and the world, the way a certain fuhrer raised a furor in what came to be known as World War II.

- To the contrary, we wish to give Mr. Moore the benefit of the doubt, considering that (1) he may feel that the ends justify the means, (2) he may have really felt that he was technically accurate in all respects—and even in his lack of respect for the president; we respect the fact that he claims to have hired lawyers to check out his facts; (3) he may really have not intended to create false, misleading, and/or otherwise unjustified material, and/or (4) he may really be imprecise, misinformed, careless, and/or not quite as bright as he would like us to think he is, all the more reason why we do not believe he should be accused of being malicious or hateful.

About the Sources

The sources utilized in this book are identified in abbreviated form in the text, as they come up, and in more detail at the conclusion of the book. The primary source is the movie itself. Many of its statements are so inherently misleading that they do not even need a formal source to be refuted; just some analysis. In a rare moment of off-screen (but on-T.V.) candor, Michael Moore himself made a statement open to the possible interpretation that he was conceding, in effect, that the movie was unfair to President Bush, or at least likely to be so interpreted. Moore observed that a poll showed that 30% of the *Republicans* who had seen the movie felt that it had treated President Bush fairly. Then he conceded, "Even I wouldn't go that far" (Moore Interview, July 30, 2004). The most powerful source that can be used to disprove much of what the movie says is the official authorized *9/11 Commission Report*, whose strengths are that it is truly bipartisan, having been authored by five Republicans and five Democrats, and that its findings are not just detailed and backed up by extensive footnotes and appendices, but also and above all that their findings are unanimous.

Honorable mention should be made of the works of Stephen Lee, Esq., of the Law Firm of Debevoise & Plimpton, LLP; Dave Kopel, director of the Independence Institute; Dr. Kelton Rhoades, adjunct professor at the University of Southern California; Lee Troxler; Justin Sayfie; the researchers of *Fahrenhype 9/11(the DVD)*, of *War, Lies, and Videotape: A Viewer's Guide to Fahrenheit 9/11 (in DVD and Internet format)*, of *Celsius 41.11 (the movie that came out about two weeks before the election)*, of *Fahrenheit* Facts Blog, Christopher Hitchen, Michael Isikoff, and Mark Hosenball, nearly all of whose works are cited with respect and appreciation in this work, and the first eight of which were consulted after I first began circulating early drafts of this work.

About the Author

Aaron Reichel, a lawyer, is a member of the federal and state bars of New York and New Jersey. He was the founder and former editor of Prentice-Hall's **Government Disclosure Service**; a charter member of the **American Society of Access Professionals**; and the founding co-chair of the New York Regional Chapter of the aforesaid Society. His focus in the latter three capacities included Freedom of Information, Privacy, and classified document data. Earlier, he served on the staff of the Advisory Committee on Court Administration of the Appellate Division of the Supreme Court of New York, and in the Environmental Protection Bureau of the Office of the Attorney General of the State of New York when the office was located in the World Trade Center.

Some of the books Reichel has authored, co-authored, or contributed to, and a small sampling of the periodicals he has written for—and of the most significant articles he has written—are listed on the back of the title page of this book. He appears in *Who's Who in the World*.

Virtual illustration of the author in a law library or surrounded with documents
or
Virtual illustration of author trying to stuff documents that don't quite fit into file cabinet, or sneaking into a file cabinet, closet, or other area, with the designation of "confidential" crossed off.

Topic 1

Tragedies Not Just of 9/11,
But Also of the *Fahrenheit 9/11* Movie

The tragedies that occurred on 9/11 are universally recognized among people who respect human life. Not as universally recognized, however, is the belief that moviegoers' responses to *Fahrenheit 9/11* also represent multi-dimensional tragedies. On one level, the tragedies of the film are that so many viewers do not realize how many of the movie's points are based on truths taken out of context, and distortions taking in gullible viewers. The greater tragedy is that the film's creator unwittingly highlights the worst danger of his movie by his boomeranging attempt to hijack the title of an earlier film, *Fahrenheit 451*, in which all books were burned, and the members of a futuristic civilization were forced to receive all of their news by watching a television or video screen rather than by reading books and newspapers. The greatest tragedy of *Fahrenheit 9/11* is that *Fahrenheit 451* is already upon us, to a great degree, except self-imposed, in that the majority of the people who will have seen *Fahrenheit 9/11* are not likely to have the patience or the inclination to read books or articles, such as this one, which expose the movie's weaknesses, point-by-point. The visual rebuttals to *Fahrenheit 9/11*—(1) *Fahrenhype—911*, (2) *War, Lies, and Videotape: A Viewer's Guide to Fahrenheit 9/11*, and (3) *Celsius 41.11*—are each arguably more informative and persuasive than *Fahrenheit 9/11*, which was too bitter, in places, to be a comedy, and too funny, in places, to be a traditional tragedy or documentary; however, the rebutting films cannot be expected to have quite the same impact as *Fahrenheit 9/11*, the full-fledged movie that filled big screens and big theatres for months before the release of the rebuttal, and for months before the Election of 2004, which effectively put an end to much of the public interest in the topic, because (1) at press time, shortly before the election of 2004, two out of three of them were only available on DVD, (2) two out of the three are not necessarily as oriented to mass markets as

Fahrenheit 9/11; many viewers may find that only *Fahrenhype 9/11* is more witty, brilliant, entertaining, and moving than *Fahrenheit 9/11*; (3) all three of the rebutting films first became available shortly before the election, (4) they did not go unresponded to on the big screen for months, prior to the election of 2004 as did *Fahrenheit 9/11*, (5) their directors are not as famous—or as infamous—as Michael Moore; (6) they did not benefit from comparable publicity, (7) they did not benefit from comparable distribution, and (8) they have not created comparable interest among people throughout the world who hate America, democracy, and the leaders of the free world.

   Virtual illustration of people watching Fahrenheit 451 *with books on fire, morphing into* Fahrenheit 9/11, *with World Trade Center on fire*
or

   Alternate virtual illustration of masked bandit hijacking a plane and grabbing a film labelled Fahrenheit 451

Topic 2

Movie Maker Moore vs. President Bush

Fahrenheit 9/11 makes President Bush appear to be not quite as intelligent, compassionate, and kind as most of us would like our president to be. Many people who read articles or books that respond to the film's points, point-by-point, with an open mind and with intellectual honesty, may easily conclude that, no matter what they may think of President Bush, as a person, or of his policies, domestic or military, Michael Moore may very possibly come across as even less intelligent, compassionate, and kind, in his portrayal of President Bush, especially as Mr. Moore drifts further from his moorings as a responsible journalist, with this movie, than with any of his previous "documentaries." This book will not argue *ad hominem*; it will not quibble about whether the film would be called, more appropriately, merely a piece of pure propaganda, and/or, to be charitable, merely a well-intentioned "mock-umentary," a "shock-umentary," or even a "schlock-umentary." Rather, it will attempt to present, either by implication or directly, both sides of every issue—Moore's and an opposing view—and leave it to the reader to evaluate them. Moore writes good comedy, at times—funny enough to make even his sharpest critics laugh in binges between cringes—but pure comedy taken seriously can lead to the ultimate tragedy, especially when the fate of the free world rests on the outcome of the presidential election that Moore is in the process of influencing in an inappropriate manner. Much more importantly, however, readers of this book or monograph—or of any other review of any length that puts virtually all of the movie's arguments and innuendoes into perspective—will be more responsible than readers who do not read such a critique, when their evaluations of this movie and of this type of a critique will be reflected in voting booths throughout the U.S.A in future elections, even if they were not exposed to such rebuttals in time for the election of 2004.

<u>Note:</u> No matter what the outcome of the Presidential election of 2004 will have been, the impact of *Fahrenheit 9/11* is sure to endure since (1) the movie is certain to have influenced record numbers of voters, (2) it is likely to be nominated for an Academy Award and to get many votes in absentia even if not nominated, and (3) its unprecedented success at the box office will guarantee its immortality and its being taken seriously among historians, politicians, and political scientists, let alone film makers and producers, for generations to come.

Many people have been wondering how it could be that so many otherwise rational and intelligent Americans have developed such a hatred of President Bush that they have compared him to Adolph Hitler, even before seeing Michael Moore's movie. One major answer is that many people believe that his policies toward the Arabs have unleashed unprecedented Muslim hatred and violence against the United States and its citizens. In response, without even touching on the points that President Bush's policies toward the Arabs have promoted freeing them from torture and tyranny (in Iraq) and from corruption and intimidation (in Palestinian-controlled territory in the Middle East), modern Muslim violence against the United States can be traced back to the regime of the Ayatollah Khomeini in Iran (*Celsius 41.11*), which began on the watch of one of the most appeasing presidents the United States ever had—Democrat Jimmy Carter.

<u>Virtual illustration</u> of Bush and Moore at the Gates of Heaven or competing in a quiz show, or two voters in the voting booth, one thinking of the movie, and one thinking of the movie review.

Topic 3

Allegations of Stolen Florida Votes Can No Longer Be Taken Seriously After Recounts

To Michael Moore's credit, he refrained from making the outrageous claim, at least in the movie, that a million African-Americans were disenfranchised by the Republican Party in Florida in the 2000 presidential election. With this reverse caveat, the rebuttal begins: Moore first sets the temeritous tone of the movie with the outdated premise that George Bush stole the presidential election in 2000. If anything, he did not steal it; at worst, it was <u>given</u> to him on a silver platter of for the most part properly confiscated ballots, delivered—but not counted—by people with possible conflicts-of-interest as to whom plausible accusations could have been—and certainly were—made at that time. What makes our democracy so special is that people have the right to challenge perceived imperfections in the system, and to have their challenges heard in a timely fashion. Ultimately, the decision that George Bush won the election was not made by his brother, Jeb, the governor of Florida, who recused himself from the governor's traditional role in the election process (Ethics & Public Policy Center, 2004), but rather at the highest levels of government, by a majority of the nine members of the U. S. Supreme Court, and by a special Joint Session of Congress presided over by the Vice-President of the United States, in this case Al Gore, the person with more of a motivation than anyone else in the world to call the election in his own favor. Nevertheless, had Moore merely alleged, in November or December of the year 2000, that Bush stole the election, the allegation still might have been made in unquestionably good faith, and it might then have been plausible and understandable; however, Moore not only re-dignifies this allegation in 2004, but goes so far as to completely ignore the findings of two large mainstream news consortiums, both benefiting from half a year of intensive recounts and investigations. The Florida Ballots Project, which will be described below, found that even had the United States Supreme Court allowed a statewide vote recount to proceed, more than was even requested by Al Gore—George Bush would still have been elected president, though by a slightly smaller margin. This is documented in the CNN Website (CNN.com), which notes that this study was conducted by the National Opinion Research Center (NORC) at the University of Chicago, for a consortium of eight news media companies including CNN, The Associated Press, The New York Times, and The Washington Post, hardly lackeys for some great amorphous "right wing conspiracy." CNN reports that the NORC "dispatched an army of trained investigators to examine closely every rejected ballot in all 67 Florida counties," on whose fact-checking it arrived at its conclusive confirmation.

Virtual illustration of people counting ballots with calendars on the wall opened to November, December, January, February, March, and April

The other consortium, headed by *USA Today* and *The Miami Herald*, specifically stated that Bush would have won even had Gore obtained the manual counts he had requested in the four counties of his choice, even had the U.S. Supreme Court not stopped the hand recount of undervotes (ballots that registered no machine-readable votes), and even had the authorities counted ballots that had been rejected because they had more than one vote for president (Lott & Blase, 2004).

When the uncounted votes are broken down by category, there were 5 major reasons why some votes were not counted—overvotes, undervotes, mistaken votes, voters not allowed to vote, and voter confusion due to media reporting (Lee, 2004). The largest category by far—over 100,000 out of about 177,500—were due to overvotes (Lee, 2004), where people voted for more than one candidate. An argument can be made that more of these voters *intended* to vote for Gore than for Bush, but elections are decided not based on what people are *thinking* when they vote, but rather on what people are *doing* when they vote—how they are *voting*. To require elections to ignore how people voted, but to base them exclusively on how they *intended* to vote is simply not practical, and was never the official criterion. The same argument can be made as to the undervotes and the mistaken votes. However, statistics have been compiled, as discussed below, indicating that the allegations of wrongdoing or error as to voters not allowed to vote and voters in the west may have actually involved more people who would have voted for *Bush* than for *Gore*!

Virtual illustration of newspapers with headlines stating "Recounts Confirm Results"

The movie makes the Fox News Network appear to be at the head of a sinister plot to turn defeat into victory for Bush, by stating that after CNN and CBS called Florida for Gore on election night, 2000, "Fox…called the election in favor of the other guy," and the rest, of course, is history (leaving out, incidentally, the fact that Fox too had originally called the state for Gore, after other networks did, and then reversed itself at about 2 A.M., about 4 hours after CNN and CBS had withdrawn their projections in favour of Gore (at about 10 P.M.)(Mason, Francovic, & Jamieson, 2001), not exactly the type of a strategy for the leader of a conspiracy on behalf of Bush. Furthermore, all the networks based their decisions on the same source—the Voting New Service, a consortium comprised of ABC, CBS, CNN, Fox, NBC, and the Associated Press (Lee, 2004). Also, John Ellis, the Bush cousin who Moore implicates in the election night confusion, did not make the final call on any election, although he did make recommendations (Lee, 2004).

Virtual illustration of TV broadcaster declaring Gore the winner, with Gore morphing into Bush.

Ironically, it has been pointed out that all the networks, including Fox, helped Gore, by (1) announcing that a Democrat had won the United States senate race in Florida an hour before the polls closed in Florida's western "panhandle" (in the Central time zone), the location of 10 heavily Republican counties, and by (2) mistakenly and falsely announcing that the Florida polls had closed at 7 P.M., Eastern time, when, in fact, polls in Florida's western panhandle were open until 7 P.M. Central time. Both of these factors encouraged Republicans in this panhandle who had not yet voted in the last hour the polls were open to give up and decide not to vote (Konner, Risser, & Wattenberg, 2001). Even the Democratic strategist Bob Beckel calculated that this early call cost Bush a net loss of up to eight thousand (8,000) votes, only about two thousand (2,000) fewer than the ten thousand (10,000) net loss calculated by John McLaughlin and Associates, a Republican polling company (Lott & Blase, 2004). Another estimate has Bush losing close to 50,000 Floridian votes as a result of the early projections of Gore winning the state before the polls had closed, presumably in other counties as well (Mauro II, 2004).

Virtual illustration of polls closing at 8, morphing into 7

Moore also alleges that George Bush's brother, Jeb, the governor of Florida, stole the election for his brother, in part by removing African-American voters, who were likely to vote for Gore, from the rolls. Facts have actually been compiled indicating to the contrary. As of the year 2000, Florida banned unpardoned felons from voting. Before the 2000 election, the state hired Database Technologies to clear the voting rolls of felons and cadavers. After some very-much-alive, innocent—and rightfully irate—non-felons were mistakenly removed, various African-Americans and their supporters cried foul; however, it turns out that even an investigation by the relatively liberal *Palm Beach Post* concluded that "a review of state records, internal e-mails of [Database Technologies], employees and testimony before the Civil Rights Commission and an elections task force showed no evidence that minorities were specifically targeted." In fact, to the contrary, a breakdown of the error rate from the rolls shows that, ironically, to the contrary, the highest error rate was for whites, and the lowest was for African-Americans (specifically, a 9.9% error rate for whites, an 8.7% error rate for Hispanics, and only a 5.1% error rate for African-Americans) (Lott & Blase, 2004).

Interestingly, the United States Civil Rights Commission, which is not likely to be dominated by a "vast right-wing conspiracy," purportedly did not find evidence of a single African-American having been turned away from the polls (*Celsius 41.11*).

Virtual illustration of four people voting simultaneously: an African-American, a very old white person, a masked person with a tattoo, and a ghost

People who allege that Database technologies was in the pocket of Republicans should note that the Palm Beach Post investigation specifically covered this company's internal e-mails, which surely would have revealed corruption or serious internal improprieties, had there been any.

Virtual illustration of somebody at a computer staring at an e-mail and saying, confidently and loudly "ah hah," with the balloon containing this statement morphing into a small and subdued, and embarrassed "huh?"

There is more. It has been found that at least 1100 people were improperly purged as felons ineligible to vote in Florida; however, they were given months to appeal, and because of the notoriety of the purges, the purge list was not used in 20 of Florida's counties, so that it has been claimed that 5,600 felons voted illegally in Florida, and felons vote, generally, about 69% Democratic (Kopel, 2004), so an argument can be made that Gore—not Bush—benefited the most from the way Florida treated its felons who wished to vote, in the year 2000.

Virtual illustration of men in striped prison uniforms getting free passes, morphing into ballots

Moore makes a spectacle of the Joint Session of Congress convened to certify the president of the United States. The defeated Vice-President Al Gore did a class act in his bitter role of presiding officer, sticking to the rules in the face of a succession of African-American members of Congress alleging irregularities in the Florida polls. The rules require at least one member of the Senate as well as of the House of Representatives, in order to make a challenge, but no senator came forth. Moore's filming such a succession of minority House members is clearly designed to make the system look ridiculous, and he likewise goes after even the liberal Democrats, his natural allies, for being too passive under the circumstances. The other side of the coin, not shown in this movie, is the low threshold required by the rules to challenge the vote—a single senator out of 100—not the 2/3 out of 100 needed to pass a treaty, or even 1/3 of 100, but just one. The fact that not even one liberal senator rose up to support the challenges, if only to pander to African-American voters, shows the depth of the senators' respect for the system that had played its course, including the rule against debates at that anticlimactic point—or there would be no end to it. The people had spoken, although Michael Moore was just beginning to get warmed up for the then-reasonable fight ahead, and for the now-unreasonable refusal to recognize the results of the unofficial recounts referred to above.

It has also been pointed out that even had one or more Senators joined in the objections at the Joint Session of Congress, they would have probably been overruled based on the rules, and had they been sustained, they would have invalidated all of Florida's votes and thrown the whole election into the House of Representatives, where Bush would have undoubtedly won anyway (Lee, 2004).

Virtual illustration of Gore presiding over Joint Session of Congress

Topic 4

Even Had the Florida Allegations Proven Correct, Did Nader Siphon Off More Votes?

We have shown, above, how even the most significant impartial and liberal widely respected entities and consortiums have determined that President Bush legitimately won the electoral votes of the crucial swing state of Florida. However, even if the critics are correct that up to tens of thousands of Floridian votes were stolen, these votes cannot compare to the votes that went to the swing candidate—Ralph Nader—not just in Florida, but across the United States. Nader won approximately 2.73% of the votes, nationwide, for a total of 2,883,105. It is the clear consensus in the political and statistical communities that although the popular vote was close, had Nader _not_ been a candidate, what would _not_ have been close is the percentage of Nader voters who would not have voted for George Bush. Most of the people who voted for Ralph Nader would have either voted against President Bush or stayed home. Perhaps the ultimate irony is conspicuously absent from Moore's analysis of the U.S. presidential election of 2000. The *coup de grace* is that Michael Moore supported Ralph Nader in that election, which means that whether or not George Bush "stole" the election from Al Gore, an argument can be made that the candidacy of Ralph Nader, as supported by Michael Moore, took away more votes from George Bush than all of the alleged irregularities in Florida combined.

Virtual illustration *of Michael Moore lifting Ralph Nader on his shoulders, while bumping into Al Gore (in effect, goring him?), and knocking him to the ground*

Alternate virtual illustration *of Gore standing tall, or on all fours like an automobile, with a pocket shaped like the gas valve of an automobile, and Michael Moore siphoning off Gore's lifeblood into the pocket of a small Ralph Nader*

Topic 5

Is Moore More Interested in Make-Up and Smiling Faces or Making Up Sad Facts?

On a personal level, Moore further sets the off-key tone of his movie by repeatedly showing the horrors of war followed by President Bush and his associates smiling, singing, or getting make-up dabbed onto their smiling faces, as if they are cruel and heartless in the face of Iraqi suffering, when it is obvious that they were <u>not</u> smiling about the suffering of innocent Iraqi civilians. While liberals are no less likely to receive a liberal amount of make-up, Moore's stooping to such a low level of persuasion, and so obsessively repeatedly, should alert viewers to the quality of his later more substantive distortions. A final observation about all this make-up is that it is far less objectionable than the way Moore may appear, to many, to <u>make up</u> outright untruths and distortions, and then to seek to swing a U.S. presidential election because so many of the viewers of his films are too naive, misinformed, and/or swept up by the illusory and contrived ironies, to see through such arguably transparent manipulative devices.

Virtual illustration of a woman patting down Bush's face with make-up, and another woman wiping the egg off the face of Moore

Topic 6

A "Vacation Day" of a President

Moore pokes fun at President Bush's superficially excessive vacation days—allegedly, 42% within his first eight months in office—which would not, incidentally, set a modern record, even if it were true (Williams, 2004). It has been noted, however, that Moore counts as vacation days, weekends, time spent at the Camp David complex, time spent at the "Texas White House" (at President Bush's Crawford Ranch), time spent at job-related events in different states, and travel time. Furthermore, even Moore's own movie suggests, indirectly, that many of those "vacation" days were working "vacation" days. The presidential vacation retreat of Camp David is now best known to the American public not for its trees or its squirrels, but rather for having been the setting for one of the most dramatic peace initiatives in modern American history, under the Democratic President Jimmy Carter, known as a workaholic and a micro-manager. It is no secret in the business world that many of the most important business deals are finalized on the golf course. Yet a golf course is where President Bush was made fun of by Moore, while Bush was interacting with Prime Minister Tony Blair, his main ally in the War on Terror, as depicted in Moore's movie (Hitchens, 2004). Moore makes fun of Bush's following a formal statement on terrorism, while on a golf course, with a rather less formal statement about his golf swing, yet this is just another indication that Bush's "vacation" days were often far from being vacations as most Americans know the term. In addition, the president always gets daily briefings, no matter where he is, with more vital information coming to his attention on a vacation day than almost every working American gets on a working day. What is more, as to President Bush's vacation day work ethic, even a *Saturday* at the ranch in August of 2001 could begin at 5:45 A.M. with daily briefs, followed by a CIA and national security briefing at 7:45 A.M., and a weekly radio address on a subject no lighter than the budget (Kopel, 2004). *FahrenHYPE* 9/11 graphically shows, on a map, a segment of President Bush's August 2001 "vacation" itinerary, crossing the United States as dramatically as the Harlem Globetrotters, while accomplishing achievements at a dizzying pace viewers are challenged to follow, much less comprehend or emulate on their "vacations."

In a single "vacation" week that August, President Bush's schedule has him appearing not just at his ranch in Texas, but also discussing the budget in Independence, Missouri, addressing a Veterans' convention in Milwaukee, answering questions from the press in Kansas City, visiting an elementary school in Crawford, speaking at the Little League World Series in Williamsport, and then at a U.S. Steel Group Steelworkers event at Mon Valley Works. On August 22, 2001, during a single "vacation" day in this week, President Bush met with Karen Hughes, Condoleezza Rice, Josh Bolten, and other staff; conferenced with Mexico's president for on (sic) Argentina's economy and IMF Role, communicated with Margaret LaMontagne on immigration policy meetings, released the Mid-Session Review, a summary of the economic outlook for the next decade, as well as of the contemporary economy and budget, announced 14 nomination and appointment intentions, issued a Presidential Determination ordering a military drawdown for Tunisia, and issued a statement regarding the retirement of Jesse Helms (www.whitehouse.gov, as cited in Troxler, 2004). Then, the *coup de grace*—all of this took place while President Bush's Washington office was being renovated (during which time he would have had to be out of the office anyway) (*Fahrenhype 9/11*). Ironically, it is now apparent that not only did President Bush not take as much vacation time as alleged, but considering his travelling schedule during this "vacation," President Bush may have actually worked HARDER on certain "vacation" days than he would have had he stayed in the White House, and with fewer "creature comforts," besides.

Virtual illustration of President Bush putting down a putter or another golf club and listening to a man in a suit pointing to a large stack of papers that the President is reaching for, to read, as he climbs steps leading into a waiting plane.

Topic 7

Are Working Vacations Necessarily Bad for People Who Delegate Effectively? What of the Alternative?

Even if Bush can be shown to spend more time on vacation than some other presidents, that in itself is not necessarily a vice if he has a competent vice president and other deputies on the job dealing with details; if it means he himself is less likely to micro-manage work more appropriately done by professional financial experts and military strategists; and if it means that he will be more likely to be alert, balanced, stable, and not overly stressed when called upon to make decisions on which the future of the free world depends. The most famous response to heavily-armed "militants" by workaholic micro-manager Jimmy Carter was a bunch of rescue helicopters helplessly grounded by a mild sandstorm which was no match for Operation Desert Storm, the latter military operation of which was fought successfully under a president not known for comparable workaholic or micro-managing tendencies.

Virtual illustration of a group of helicopters grounded by a sandstorm in the middle of a desert

Topic 8

Criticism of Bush's Failure to Make a Sudden Grand Exit on 9/11

Moore makes fun of President Bush's failure to take immediate action after hearing of the plane crashes on 9/11; Bush's remaining for a few minutes at a scheduled kindergarten class visit; and picking up a book featuring, *inter alia*, the now-most-famous goat in America, although it turns out, incidentally, that the book he picked up did not even have the word "goat" in its title (as further detailed below). For the record, President Bush remained there for 5 minutes, not 7 (*Fahrenhype 9/11*, 2004). Moore clearly relishes the opportunity to show the president's poker-faced demeanor at the time, and to speculate comically as to what the president was thinking. Moore suggests that the President may have been thinking that he should have read a certain presidential briefing about bin Ladin having at some point planned to attack America by hijacking planes, although Moore provides no evidence that the President had not in fact read that briefing, which he was presumed to have read since it had been prepared specifically for him. In the process of Moore's undocumented speculation as to what President Bush might have been thinking, Moore blocked out of his viewers' consciousnesses the following thoughts that should have been going through *their* minds at the time, in no particular order: (1) The identity of the entity responsible for the crashes was not immediately established conclusively. Some people are debating it to this day. After the first World Trade Center attack, on February 26, 1993, the focus of the Clinton administration was on convicting the immediate perpetrators of the crime; not on retaliating against the underlying masterminds and their hordes of lemming-like followers. After the Cole attack on October 12, 2000, not only did President Clinton fail to swing into action with immediate retaliation, but he could have read numerous full-length *books* for *grown-ups* about entire farms of barnyard animals in the time it took his administration to figure out who was to blame, and how to respond. It never even conclusively blamed al Qaeda (*9/11 Commission Report*, p. 193), and therefore never retaliated (*9/11 Commission Report*, p. 191), let alone did it launch the all-out offensive that could have prevented the 9/11 attacks; instead, the Clinton administration left the heavily-armed "militant" problem squarely in Bush's lap when he took office. (2) Effective leadership often entails projecting a sense of calm in the face of a crisis, let alone in the focus of many poised cameras. And this is precisely what President Bush was thinking, moments after the second tower was hit, on 9/11 (*9/11 Commission Report*, p.38); not the goat. (3) Even routine facts, let alone unprecedented and highly ambiguous ones, have to be marshalled, analyzed, and then presented to the president before retaliation can be begun. (4) President Bush could not have gone anywhere, right away, anyway, without his staff first working out logistics and deciding where to advise the president to go, in conjunction with the Secret Service detail, which always has to plan ahead for his every move. (5) This was especially necessary and significant in light of a *Washington Times* story stating that, on the morning of September 11th, a Middle Eastern man had tried to penetrate the Secret Service to gain direct access to the president under false pretenses, with precise knowledge of the name of one of the Secret Service agents (Kopel, 2004). (5) For this reason, one of the president's aides held up a large sign, telling the president not to move yet, and footage of the kindergarten visit shows the president nodding, almost imperceptibly, with his approval (*Fahrenhype 9/11*) (6) President Bush's actions, or lack of apparent action, weren't criticized, at the time, by the media at the scene (*Fahrenhype 9/11*); (7) his actions were even praised by the African-American principal, Florida Gore supporter Gwen Tose-Rigell (*Fahrenhype 9/11*); (8) had Bush immediately jumped into action—or reaction—he would undoubtedly have been accused by Moore as having projected an aura of being unprepared, overwhelmed, impulsive, predisposed to react, and/or over-eager to micro-manage the crisis or to grandstand with a "photo-op" within a "photo-op" in an instant response (some of which accusations Moore of course makes anyway); (9) Moore also leaves out the brief historical fact that the President *did* decide to make a brief statement while still at the school in Florida moments later, and followed through with a speech to the nation while still in the Florida schoolhouse (*9/11 Commission Report*, p. 39; *Fahrenhype 9/11*). So this is another indication that it was *not* the goat that was on President Bush's mind as he prepared to speak extemporaneously moments later. (10) Furthermore, in less than half an hour, President Bush had already spoken to some of his close national security people, including his National Security Adviser Condoleezza Rice and FBI Director Robert Mueller (Lee, 2004) and told Vice-President Cheney "We're at war...somebody's going to pay" (*9/11 Commission Report*, p. 39). Unlike President Clinton after the first World Trade

Center attack and after the Cole attack, Bush made sure the people behind the perpetrators would pay, in a big way, and with relatively minimal delay. A final thought about poker faces: Moore can poke as much fun as he wants at President Bush, but it is the poker player with the best poker face who generally wins. <u>Now</u> who is the "goat" in this context?

<u>Virtual illustration</u> of President Bush playing poker around a small table. A goat with Michael Moore's untrimmed beard and trademark hat is chewing some of the chips off the table

Topic 9

What Did Bush Know, and When Did He Know It?

Moore implies that Bush should have known, in advance, that planes piloted by heavily-armed "militants" would come crashing into buildings on or around 9/11, based on a presidential daily briefing given to him August 6, 2001, that a claim had been made but not corroborated that bin Laden had been planning, as of 1998 (during President Clinton's term), to hijack air planes; however, even this briefing did not necessarily suggest that the prospective hijackers planned to *pilot* the planes, nor that they were planning to do so into civilian, financial, political, and/or military targets. Moore makes it seem like Dr. Condoleezza Rice, Bush's National Security Advisor, did not focus on this warning since the title of the briefing was vague, when in fact she was referring to the *contents* of the briefing that were vague (Kopel, 2004), and that fell short of indicating that the hijackers intended to *pilot* the planes into specific targets. It is true that, somewhere among the hundreds of threats intercepted by the U.S. government routinely, but at a relatively low level in the chain of intelligence briefings, mention was made of such a possibility. The 9/11 Commission found that a memo from a single FBI agent warning of the possibility of plans by Bin Ladin to send members of al Qaeda to flight schools was not widely circulated within the FBI and never was brought to the attention of John Ashcroft, much less to the attention of the president (*9/11 Commission Report*).

It should also be kept in mind that the head of the CIA on 9/11 was George Tenet, a holdover from the Clinton Administration, and the Chief of Counterterrorism was Richard Clarke, another Clinton holdover (notwithstanding his original appointment). To be sure, they were not the only Clinton holdovers, nor were they the only highly-trained professionals to be caught off-guard on 9/11, although Clarke was clearly more pro-active than most. So was President

Bush himself, at whose initiative the briefing on August 6, 2001 was prepared, and whose personal concern about Bin Laden in particular was highlighted by his spokesman Ira Fleisher June 27, 2001 (Lee, 2004).

Virtual illustration of President Bush's appointment book with an entry for 9/11 showing jets with hijacking pilots, and Bush saying to Moore, who has a pen in his hand, "I know these were not on my guest list"

Incidentally, Moore makes a point of saying that Attorney General John Ashcroft said he didn't want to know details about terrorist threats. First of all, Mr. Ashcroft denies this allegation vehemently (*9/11 Commission Report*, p. 265). Secondly, the man who gave Ashcroft his briefings, Acting FBI director Thomas Pickard, testified that even though Ashcroft told him he didn't want to receive any more briefings after the second one, Pickard continued to give them (*9/11 Commission Report*, p. 265), which calls into question the original accusation. Would Ashcroft—or anyone in a position of authority—listen to briefings he or she did not want to hear? But even if it were true, if John Ashcroft, who was not a Clinton holdover, did not wish to be peppered with details about terrorist threats, at some point, could it be because the role of the attorney general is not supposed to be to micro-manage or to do the work of the CIA, the FBI, and the National Security Advisor? Their counterterrorism attitudes and efforts are described in some detail, below.

Virtual illustration of Attorney General John Ashcroft pushing aside a crystal ball, and studying a thick briefing book.

Topic 10

Was Pre-2003 Iraq
Really a Happy Utopia?

Viewers of the movie who have been living on Mars or in what some would say is Moore's comparably unearthly world would believe that until the United States invasion in 2003, the typical Iraqi was so carefree and happy that his biggest challenge in life was keeping his kite from getting entangled around satellite dishes. Moore's portrayal of Iraq as a cheerful and utopian paradise was pointedly singled out for condemnation not once but twice by Senator McCain at the 2004 Republican convention, a former prisoner of war who knows what regimes like Saddam Hussein's are *really* like. The movie makes virtually no mention of Saddam's unspeakable crimes against humanity that were outrageous even by the standards of many other authoritarian countries. It is not necessary to delineate them here; we assume that virtually everyone in the universe of the free world, except, perhaps, Michael Moore, needs no documentation on this point. Whether the war was begun with the proper motives, justifications, precautions, inspections, and coalition may be subject to debate, but to make it seem like the citizens of Iraq would be far better off under the ante-bellum status quo of rule by Saddam Hussein is an insult to the intelligence of every viewer, as is the implication that the United States targeted civilians.

Virtual illustration of a kite entangled in a satellite dish, on a sunny side of a wall, while the string of the kite extends over the wall to a cloudy scene, and serves as a noose around the neck of an Iraqi citizen on the cloudy side of the wall.

Topic 11

Did the United States Really Make Saddam Look Like a Civil Rights Pussycat?

Fahrenheit 9/11 makes it seem as if the United States destroyed this apparent utopia, crashing into apparent civilian residences and places of entertainment. This is particularly outrageous considering that Moore portrays civilian victims of American military might without a single reference to the high-tech "smart bombs" and other weaponry that was responsible for the <u>lowest percentage of civilian casualties</u>, compared to military and strategic casualties, <u>in the history of warfare</u>. The Americans' care in surgically shooting around—and not at—civilian targets, instead of just bombing whole areas from a distance, cost American lives, contrasting with the Iraqis' approach to human life, where they purposely embedded military installations in civilian areas and used civilians as human shields. Moore's misplaced sense of immoral equivalence fails to contrast American regret over even the relatively few civilian injuries they inflicted, against, by contrast, Saddam's knowing murders and tortures of so many hundreds of thousands of his own civilians in the course of his despotic rule, and many of Saddam's followers dancing in the streets every time a suicide bomber commits mass murder.

Virtual illustration of smart bomb zigzagging around civilians, while Saddam is torturing his own people e

Topic 12

Evidence Shows No Saudi Bribe, and No Conspiracy

Moore takes great pains to allege that after George W. Bush missed a physical at the Texas Air National Guard decades ago at the same time as another young man named James R. Bath did so, Bath's name was later blocked out of government records on the subject allegedly because he once served as the money manager for the Bin Ladin family and then allegedly channelled money into one of Bush's companies. In fact, Bath's name was blocked out at the time Moore made his movie because the government was required to block it out, by a law—the Health Insurance Portability and Accountability Act (HIPAA)—that was passed after Michael Moore obtained a copy of the file without the blockage before that law had been passed. Furthermore, it is true that Mr. Bath missed a physical exam at approximately the same time as a young George Bush did, and eventually worked for the Bin Ladins in America (Isikoff & Hosenball), but working with relatives of a criminal who is virtually incommunicado on another continent and in another world does not make every investor and/or employee into a co-conspirator with the criminal on the other side of the globe. T.he U.S. government was well aware of the Bin Ladins who ran one of Saudi Arabia's biggest construction firms, which had never been linked to terrorism, throughout the Clinton years. The U. S. government had ample opportunity to scrutinize their possible links in America to Usama in Afghanistan as much as it deemed necessary. Yet with all of this, no credible evidence was offered to substantiate the above innuendo that Bath funnelled Bin Ladin money into a Bush company. To the contrary, Moore carefully phrased his words to the effect that "Bath invested in George Bush." Moore doesn't even technically allege that Bath put any Bin Ladin money into any George Bush company. And Bath vehemently denies that the money that he invested in one of Bush's companies had any link to Bin Ladin's companies

(Isikoff & Hosenball), yet Moore insists on giving the facts a bath, so to speak, in filthy water, and on attempting to sully Bush's reputation in the process.

Virtual illustration of man with a torso of a bath tub or a man in a bath tub giving President Bush money, while Saudis dressed like Arab old-timers look the other way, and Bin Ladin is shown in the distance, looking the other way.

Topic 13

Do Saudis and Bush Have Each Other in Their Respective Pockets?

The insinuation that the Saudis run U.S. policy, with Bush under their thumbs or around their other fingers, is rebutted by the facts, *inter alia*, that President Bush's positions on Israel's right to defend itself are far from the Saudis', and the Saudis officially opposed the ongoing wars against the heavily-armed "militants" of Afghanistan and Iraq to the point where they officially ejected and kicked out American soldiers and officially did not even allow American planes to use many of their American-built and staffed sophisticated military facilities, let alone their soldiers (although the Saudis' public rhetoric was worse than their actual deeds). The very fact that Bush has emphasized his interest in promoting democracy throughout the Arab world, post 9/11, might be the strongest indication of all that he is not beholden to the royal House of Saud, which is quite satisfied with the political status quo, in its kingdom. Moore points out the tremendous financial investments the Saudis had in the United States at the start of the War, as if somehow this was all Bush's "fault," possibly just to buy his good will.

Nobody with even a minimal knowledge of world affairs disputes that the Saudis have been investing heavily in the United States for many consecutive administrations, Democratic as well as Republican. The Saudis have supported administration officials of both parties, directly and/or indirectly, in many ways, when they were in office as well as out of it. The presidential libraries and centers of Presidents Clinton and Carter, for example, are doing very well by Saudi Arabian donations.

Moore states that the Saudis invested 860 billion dollars in the United States, and a trillion dollars in our banks. Although these statistics seem inconsistent (how can the Saudis have more money in one industry than in all industries combined?—unless the calculations include the foreign assets of the American banks), independently or together the statistics actually work in favor of what Bush has been doing by his cultivating the cooperation and friendship of the Saudis, in general, when not in conflict with our values and interests. Were the Saudis to suddenly pull out their investments or stop the flow of oil, the repercussions to the United States could be calamitous, so that staying on good terms with the Saudis serves the interests of the United States far more than it could serve the interests of Presidents Bush, past and present, whose income potentials are unlimited, and who are free, when not in public office, to invest, advise, or consult virtually anywhere, who have no problems filling their respective cars with gas, and whose dependence on Saudi oil and investments cannot begin to compare to the dependence of the United States on the Saudis.

Note: Although there is a law allowing the president of the United States to prevent a sudden withdrawal of all Saudi investments, if the president were to do so, he would in all likelihood indirectly cause other countries and their nationals to pull out substantial investments from the United States (Lee, 2004), in which case the indirect results could be just as devastating as the withdrawals prevented by the law.

If the U.S. Secret Service protects the Saudi embassy in Washington, D. C., as portrayed in the film, it can easily be deemed to be money well spent, and not conspiratorially spent, since the good will of this country is vital, right now, to our economy, and without our economy, there would be no military to protect us. Moreover, the Saudis, with no fanfare, generally support our military by allowing our bases to operate in their country even though many of their citizens oppose such an arrangement and even though many experts believe that one of al Qaeda's raisons d'etre is to fight foreign placement on Saudi soil. The Saudis also can be helpful behind the scenes, as when, for example, they quietly disrupted Bin Ladin cells in their country that had planned to attack United States forces with shoulder-fired missiles, even during the Clinton administration, in 1998 (*9/11 Commission Report*, p. 115).

All of this having been said in justification of protecting the Saudi embassy, the fact is that the United States Secret Service protects <u>all</u> foreign embassies that request it, and not just as a down payment for presidential library donations. The Geneva Convention requires all host countries to provide protection for all embassies within their borders.

Virtual fuzzy illustration of Bush with his hand in Saudi's back pocket, and of Saudi with his hand in Bush's back pocket, with the caption, "Only in Michael Moore's Dreams—and Films."

Topic 14

Is Our Real Enemy in the White House or in the Heartland, As Implied?

Moore's suggestion that the U.S. should not have fought Iraq because the real enemy was in Afghanistan is belied by links between the "militant" entities referred to below, and by Moore's views elsewhere in the film that the *real* enemy is in the White House, and Saddam and his cohorts are the ones who deserve our sympathy and empathy. Rather than acknowledge that Saddam had tortured and murdered hundreds of thousands of his own innocent people, Moore states, at one particularly bizarre point in his movie, that Bush's next target was the American people—as if somehow President Bush launched his War on Terror to be fought against <u>his</u> own people.

It is true that the Patriot Act authorizes the United States government to set up surveillance on Americans in order to enable it to locate heavily-armed "militants'" cells and *supporters,* and that some of the surveillance may not have followed up the most promising leads, as shown in the movie's scene of rather unthreatening-looking cookie-munching suspects. However, the questions present themselves to whether (1) there was reason to believe that any of the cookie munchers were also numbers crunchers or supporters of pilot punchers, in indirect financial or other support of the "militants," and/or (2) whether it would be worthwhile to incon-venience—but *not* harm or torture—999 out of 1000 innocent people for the 1 in 1000 searches that might lead to the apprehension of people linked to al Qaeda cells who could perpetuate another conventional 9/11-type attack, or worse (one involving weapons of mass destruction—WMD), even if some of the searches (far closer to 1 than to 1000) will be conducted by overzealous or even stupid FBI agents?

Even if some innocent people will inevitably be temporarily detained for ques-tioning when suspicions might be aroused at various checkpoints, meetings, libraries, or Internet sites, for example, there is little doubt that most people think the inconvenience is worthwhile. Even the liberal Democratic Senator Diane Feinstein has been quoted as being at least indirectly in support of this assessment, following a query she had posed to the American Civil Liberties Union, eliciting the revelation that they couldn't cite a single case in which anyone's rights had actually been taken away because of the implementation of the Patriot Act (cited by former New York City Mayor Ed Koch, in Troxler, 2004).

Virtual illustration of Moore pointing at a cookie-muncher in the Midwest of a map of the United States, George Bush in the White House on this same map, and Hamid Karzai (but not the Taliban) on a map of Afghanistan (all three labelled "the enemy"), while Saddam Hussein looks on, from a prison cell, and Usama Bin Ladin look on, from a cave, with puzzled expressions.

Topic 15

Bush Influence with Saudis Eclipsed by Surprising Alternative

Moore's claim that the Saudis gave $1.4 billion to the Bush *family* (emphasis and priority given in the film), friends, and related businesses should be considered in the context that $1.18 billion of this money was not <u>given</u> to the Bushes, *et al.*, but was <u>paid</u> for services rendered by a company called BDM, a U.S. defense contractor owned by the Carlyle Group, whose advisory board former President George Bush did not join until April, 1998, five months after Carlyle had already sold BDM to another defense firm, according to Carlyle spokesperson Chris Ullman (Isikoff & Hosenball, 2004). The younger George Bush had resigned from the board of Caterair (another Carlyle subsidiary) a few months before the first of the Saudi contracts to the unrelated BDM firm was awarded (Isikoff & Hosenball, 2004), and, of course, did not become president until 2001. What is more, this contract was awarded for the training of the military and the National Guard, having nothing to do with oil. Finally, note that the deal was consummated during the <u>Clinton</u> administration. And many high-profile members of the Clinton administration were also affiliated with this company, at various times, so it was clearly bipartisan. The firm's senior advisors include Thomas "Mack" McLarty," Clinton's former White House Chief of Staff, and Arthur Levitt, the former Securities and Exchange Commission (SEC) chair under Clinton. One of its managing partners is William Kennard, the chair of the Federal Communications Commission in the Clinton Administration. Even Carlyle's spokesman, Chris Ullman, just quoted above, had been a Clinton administration spokesperson for the SEC (Isikoff and Hosenball, 2004). What is more, President George W. Bush's administration cancelled an eleven billion dollar program for a rocket system that had been developed by this company during the <u>Clinton</u> administration (Isikoff and Hosenball, 2004). If anything, an argument can be made that Carlyle may have had—and now may have—more of Clinton's high-profile people than Bush's. To top it off, and to update all of the above, President Bush's primary financial adversary, whose avowed main remaining goal in life is to push President Bush out of office with an avalanche of money—George Soros (the anti-George)—has reputedly invested in Carlyle as well (Rhoades, 2004).

It has also been calculated by one of Moore's own primary sources (Unger, 2004) that Saudi Arabia has contributed eight times as much to President Bill Clinton's charities than to the charities of President George H. W. Bush (Lee, 2004).

Virtual illustration of Arabs hugging *Clinton* advisors

In addition, Moore ingenuously compares income to the Bush family, friends, and related businesses from Saudi Arabia, to George Bush's income as president of the United States, and then comically and facetiously asks "Who's your Daddy?" This is not a fair question or comparison. If one compares what Saudi Arabia paid to the Bush family, friends, and related businesses, against what the United States did, one finds that the United States paid to a single company—Carlyle—nearly 4 billion dollars in one 4-year period, more than double the 1.4 billion dollars Moore claims Saudi Arabia paid to Bush's entire family friends, and related businesses (Lee, 2004), and this doesn't even count all other United States payments to all other friends and companies with ties to the Bushes, nor does it count the Bushes' cumulative government salaries, benefits, pensions, matching campaign contributions, and presidential library support.

Virtual illustration of a bigger funnel from the United States than from Saudi Arabia, leading into the pockets of Presidents Bush and other people and companies

Topic 16

Was Iraq Truly Sovereign when the Second Gulf War Began?

Moore solemnly refers to pre-9/11 Iraq as a sovereign nation, which places him in an outdated time warp once again. In fact, Iraq's pre-Gulf-War-II sovereignty was significantly compromised and limited by United Nations resolutions following the original Gulf War of 1991, and Saddam's premeditated repeated failures to live up to the terms of his surrender, resulting in sanctions such as the restriction on Iraq's ability to sell its main product—oil—except within the framework of the now-discredited oil-for-food (OFF) program, and also resulting in no-fly zones preventing Saddam from even entering the airspace over major segments of his own territory (Hitchens, 2004).

Virtual illustration of American planes flying over Northern and Southern sections of Iraq, with oil being filtered through the United Nations into cash in Saddam Hussein's pockets, and gold in his palaces.

Topic 17

Could a Weakened Saddam Have Still Been Dangerous?

Moore cites Colin Powell and Condoleezza Rice as stating, respectively, prior to 9/11, that Saddam had not developed significant capabilities regarding weapons of mass destruction, and the U.S. was able to keep arms from him. The implication was that these U.S. high officials denied prior to 9/11 that Iraq had such weapons, and therefore undercut the primary justification for the U.S. to lead a coalition into a war. As to the first statement, since nobody disputes that Saddam had developed weapons of mass destruction before the first war, this statement could only have reasonably been interpreted to mean that Saddam had not developed significant WMD capabilities after the first war, which is perfectly consistent with the U.S. position all along, that we were concerned that Saddam had not accounted for the WMD he had accumulated prior to the first Gulf War, and therefore was a threat to use or share these WMD in the second Gulf war or at any other time, and of course to build new ones after sanctions would be lifted. Furthermore, Powell's statement referred to above followed up his declaration that sanctions had worked, and sanctions were applied after Saddam's original WMD had been assembled.

The statement that the U.S. was able to keep arms from Saddam does not say or mean that Saddam had no arms; rather, it was obviously meant to say that he had not acquired *new* arms of any significance after the first Gulf War. Once again, the U.S. position all along, prior to the second Gulf War, was that Saddam simply had to account for his old existing WMD, and then the U.S. would have favored lifting sanctions. Saddam's failure to do so in a meaningful way cost him his freedom and his country.

Virtual illustration of a time-line showing WMD being assembled and shown on a map prior to the first Gulf War, and being hidden and shipped out of the country between the 2 wars.

Topic 18

Had Saddam Hussein Really Never Posed a Threat to the United States?

Moore states that the United States had no justification to attack Iraq since, *inter alia*, Iraq under Saddam as a country had purportedly never attacked the United States or even threatened the United States, nor had Saddam's Iraq even murdered a single United States citizen, according to Moore. At the outset, it may be noted that it is preferable to pre-empt certain attack than to wait for it to come. Even Premier Vladimir Putin's Russians, who argued against the United States' pre-emptive attack on Iraq, had warned the Americans prior to 9/11 that they (the Russians) had received intelligence of a planned Iraq attack on the United States (Gingrich Interview, 2004). More indirectly, but also more concretely, Iraq's invasion of Kuwait precipitating the first Gulf War may not have been a formal invasion of the United States, but it certainly posed a threat to the security of the United States, because Kuwait was a valuable ally of the United States, and had Saddam then proceeded into Saudi Arabia, and prevented us or our allies from getting any access to the oil of these three leading oil-producing countries, and possibly others, we could have been brought to our knees as a nation—and not to pray or to propose. Saddam's blood-curdling threats against the Coalition that he faced in both Gulf wars were made, of course, primarily against American soldiers, hundreds of thousands of whom were stationed in harm's way the first time around. Does anyone seriously deny Saddam's attempt to kill not just any American but a former president of the United States? (Incidentally, Clinton's stated desire to have Bin Ladin killed—*9/11 Commission Report*, p. 133—might be seen in perspective of the fact that Clinton himself was a target of al Qaeda plans to personally assassinate him in 1994—*9/11 Commission Report*, p. 147 refers to the targeting; not to the speculation as to a possible additional—not foremost—motive to retaliate, similar to George W. Bush's possible additional—and not foremost—motive)

Can anyone seriously deny Saddam's forces' <u>daily</u> shooting at American aircraft in the no-fly zones over his country for many <u>years</u>? Is there any informed person in the world who can seriously deny Saddam's harboring of—and thereby encouraging and supporting—mass-murdering heavily-armed "militants" associated with hijacking planes and bombing airports servicing Americans long before many of the 9/11 victims were even born, as well as Saddam's providing refuge to a heavily-armed "militant" who had been involved in the original World Trade Center attack of 1993 (Hitchens, 2004)? There is evidence that Ramzi Yousef, the ringleader of the World Trade Center bombings in 1993, not only received refuge in Iraq but also was working for Iraq's intelligence service (Mylroi, 2001). Similarly, a Mr. Yasin not only received refuge in Iraq but also helped mix chemicals for the bomb used in the World Trade Center in 1993 (Kopel, 2004). What of Saddam's open support of the families of suicide bombers who killed many Americans (and whose families received $25,000 per hit, from his regime, as a further inducement and incentive) outside of the United States, but who by no means excluded Americans as targets? (If anything, a restaurant like Sbarro's, with an American name, was more likely than not, to have Americans as employees or patrons.) Although Moore may argue that some of these instances involve Iraqis as mere accessories to crimes or harboring perpetrators after the facts of the murders, the funding of suicide bombers was so well known that they had to have served as inducements to participate in suicide bombings, rendering Iraq an accessory, many times over, *before* the facts and the dastardly acts.

Virtual illustration of Saddam Hussein as an angel sending love letters to the United States.

Topic 19

Were There Really No Pre-9/11 Links Between Saddam and Al Qaeda?

There is another consideration in response to Moore's claim that the United States was unjustified in attacking Iraq. Even if it were true that, as alleged by Moore, Iraq had never attacked or even threatened the United States, it is unquestionably true that there were connections and friendly contacts between al Qaeda and Saddam Hussein's government before 9/11 (*9/11 Commission Report*, p. 66). The Commission merely did not find conclusive evidence of a cooperative or collaborative operational relationship with regard to attacks on the United States, per se (*9/11 Commission Report*, p. 66), although a non-aggression pact between the two entities has been reported (Hayes, 2004).

An entire book has been written, documenting links between the two entities (*Hayes,* 2004). Especially noteworthy are the many links between the two entities dealing with weapons of mass destruction, at various times in the 1990s, as noted not just by right-wing activists but also by Justice Department personnel during the Clinton administration. Evidence has been accumulated showing al Qaeda members training and receiving military assistance in Iraq at various times, most ominously and significantly in 2001. Even the Bush-Bashing darling of the left, Richard Clarke himself, cited Iraqi links to al Qaeda to justify moves against Iraq in the late 1990s (Mauro II, 2004).

Notwithstanding the natural coolness that generally prevailed between the fanatically religious Usama Bin Ladin and the secularist and hedonistic Saddam Hussein, at times their common hatred of the Americans brought them together. After Bin Ladin's February 23, 1998 public fatwa (Declaration of War) against the United States, Iraq actually took the initiative in seeking cooperation with Bin Ladin (*9/11 Commission Report*, p. 66). In March, 1998, al Qaeda members met with Iraqi intelligence in Iraq, and in July of that year, an Iraqi delegation met with Bin Ladin in Afghanistan (*9/11 Commission Report*, p. 66). It was during this summer that al Qaeda began direct attacks on U.S. embassies (*9/11 Commission Report*, p. 67). Whether there is any connection between these meetings and these attacks is not spelled out in the *Report*, but the *Report* does nothing to rule out the possibility. It is also most noteworthy that Iraqi officials even went so far as to reportedly offer Bin Ladin a safe haven in Iraq (*9/11 Commission Report*, p. 66 and p. 134). The reader can judge the significance of the fact that this offer took place within about a year after Bin Ladin's public Declaration of War against the United States, to which he urged all to join.

Virtual illustration of *Saddam Hussein and Usama Bin Ladin with arms around each other's shoulders, and with big smiles.*

Topic 20

Didn't the United States Coddle Saddam Hussein as Recently as in the 1980s?

It is true that the United States supported Saddam Hussein in the 1980s, but only to the extent Iraq was in effect fighting our war against Iran, a worse enemy, on our behalf, and taking far more casualties instead of us than we have incurred in both of our wars against Iraq and in the aftermath of both wars. For this, all Americans should be grateful, instead of blaming Rumsfeld and others for prior dealings with Iraq. The United States was under no illusions that Saddam was a Saint, or even a decent human being, but even bacteria or manure can sometimes be helpful, if not even essential, to the chain of life.

Virtual illustration of the United States giving the Iraqis weapons, which were then immediately put in use against the Iranians.

Topic 21

Would the U.S. Have Gone After Saddam Even Without 9/11?

The Senate unanimously passed the Iraq Liberation Act in October of 1998, making it the official policy of the United States to seek regime change in Iraq. What is noteworthy about this piece of legislation is that it happened when President *Clinton* was in office, it had the unanimous support of even every Democratic Senator, and it was passed long before 9/11. In other words, the United States was satisfied that it had enough independent reasons to unseat Saddam Hussein even had 9/11 never occurred, and even had he had no links to al Qaeda. It also means that if President Bush came into office with an agenda to go after Saddam Hussein, it wasn't quite as personal and sinister an agenda as Moore and many of President Bush's other critics perhaps sinfully insinuate.

In *Fahrenheit 9/11*, Moore refers to the evidence against al Qaeda, and then insinuates that President Bush then concluded, irrationally, and even comically, to place the blame for 9/11 on Saddam. It may be true that President Bush made no secret of the fact that he *hoped* he would find a smoking gun in Saddam's hand, but the facts are that President Bush followed the evidence and went after al Qaeda first, in response to 9/11. Only after flushing most of al Qaeda out of Afghanistan did he get back to finishing President Clinton's work and implementing the Iraq Liberation Act of 1998.

Virtual illustration of Clinton and a united Senate pointing with weapons at Saddam Hussein, and motioning him to go out the nearest door.

Topic 22

Should the United States Have Held Out for More Votes in the United Nations?

Evidence has been mounting, for years, that Saddam Hussein was bribing officials in key veto-wielding countries in the United Nations, with oil-for-food money stolen from the starving people for which it was intended, so that the countries they represented would never vote to continue with the sanctions. Specifically, Saddam Hussein spent $10,000,000,000.00 (ten BILLION dollars) that have already been accounted for, bribing top officials of France, Germany, and Russia for this purpose (Troxler, 2004). Who knows how much more was spent for this purpose, considering that this figure was arrived at <u>before</u> the Duelfer Report (2004) which was dated September 30, which was released to the public in a very public manner on October 7, 2004, and which spelled out the names of French officials and companies on the take, including a former French interior minister and an official of a French petroleum company said to be close to the President of France. The report implicated the Russians very heavily as well, since both of these countries have vetoes in the Security Council. And the report refers to a list published in January 2004 by a Baghdad newspaper including 200 names of people from 40 countries (a loose Coalition of the Sinning which was larger than President Bush's coalition of the Willing) who allegedly peddled influence with Iraq in return for export vouchers for millions of barrels of oil to be sold for huge profits (AFP, 2004). People who were bribed would probably not have been very likely to base their votes to authorize a war in Iraq, or to send troops to keep the peace, based on who would occupy the Oval Office. So All arguments that the United States should have held out for future United Nations votes on sanctions are now proven to have been worthless.

It may also be worth noting that even when the United States offered to cooperate with the United Nations, to help build the peace after the war, the United

Nations showed its collective reliability by pulling out its troops after a single attack. The United Nations sent fewer people to Iraq to help prepare for elections than it has sent for this purpose to smaller nations that most people never heard of. And even in Afghanistan, where the United Nations are far more united than they have been about Iraq, they have not even managed to keep their commitments (*Celsius 41.11*), much less to do more than the minimum.

To those who point out that violence never solved anything, the American people did not wrest their future country from the British by merely throwing tea into a harbour; the world did not stop Hitler by appeasing him as the British originally did at that time, or by burying its head in the sand as the French did at that time; the world stopped Hitler by force, and would have prevented the deaths of millions of innocent people had it resorted to force earlier (Medved, in *Celsius 41.11*).

Virtual illustration showing Saddam accepting money which was supposed to pay for oil to be spent on food, funnelling it, instead, into the pockets of Frenchmen, Germans, and Russians.

Topic 23

Was Anybody Ever Listening to Richard Clarke? Was the Clinton Administration the Only One Listening?

As Clarke and Moore would have it, Clarke and his terrorism warnings were taken seriously only by the Clinton administration, and not by the Bush administration. To the contrary, the *9/11 Commission Report* makes it quite clear that the counter-terrorist agencies in *both* administrations generally did not understand the seriousness of the threats, and did not adjust their policies, plans, and practices to deter or defeat them (*9/11 Commission Report*, p. xvi).

Al Qaeda struck the United States with comparable ease and devastation at the beginning of the Clinton Administration (at the World Trade Center in 1993) and at the end (at the U.S. Cole, in 2000). Clark admitted that even had his policy advice been accepted immediately and turned into action by the Bush administration, it would not have prevented 9/11 (*9/11 Commission Report*, p. 348).

<u>*Virtual illustration*</u> *of Clinton and his people, and Bush and his people, looking the other way as heavily-armed "militants" acted menacingly.*

Topic 24

Did Bush and his Administration Ignore al Qaeda Threats Prior to 9/11?

Moore's claim that President Bush and his Administration ignored the threats posed by al Qaeda prior to 9/11 are rebutted by the 9/11 Commission's references to the contrary, most notably at virtually each page from 198 to 214 (*9/11 Commission Report*, pp. 198–214), notwithstanding Clarke's about-face and Bush-bashing complaints after he was retained by the Bush administration as a Clinton holdover, and then later reassigned, which [complaints] should be taken with a grain of salt for this reason. Furthermore, the Bush administration had developed and already begun to implement a long-term plan to pressure the Taliban to hand over Bin Laden to the United States prior to 9/11 (Lee, 2004).

President Bush received daily briefings from George Tenet, the head of the CIA (*9/11 Commission Report*, p. 263). In addition, there were no fewer than 40 full-blown intelligence articles in the CIA-authored President's Daily Brief (PDF) relating to Bin Ladin from January 20 to September 10, 2001 (*9/11 Commission Report*, p. 254). President Bush was alert to the sweeping or general nature of the al Qaeda threats ascribed to him, and pointedly asked, on several occasions during the spring and summer of 2001, whether any of the threats pointed to the United States. As a result, the 36th PDB that year, on August 6, 2001, entitled "Bin Ladin determined to strike in U.S," became the first to focus on the threat to the U.S. homeland (*9/11 Commission Report*, p. 260). This is mentioned here to show how, if anything, President Bush may have been more concerned about a direct attack on the U.S. mainland than some of his aides; it is *not* intended to show that the U.S. intelligence community was not acting on threats to the homeland, since this was *not* the case. To the contrary, President Bush later told the 9/11 Commission that he was well aware of Bin Ladin's long-standing desire to attack America, and recalled thinking that "it was heartening that 70 [full field

FBI] investigations" of the threats from Al Qaeda were underway (*9/11 Commission Report*, p. 260). When reports did not specify where threatened attacks were to take place, FBI officials presumed that they would continue to be overseas, although "**they did not rule out a target in the United States. Each of the FBI threat advisories made this point**" (italics and bold-face font added) (*9/11 Commission Report*, p. 263). Condoleezza Rice told the Commission that "she understood that the FBI had tasked its 56 U.S. field offices to increase surveillance of suspected terrorists and to reach out to informants who might have information about terrorist plots" (*9/11 Commission Report*, p. 264). On March 30, 2001, the CIA issued and cabled an "Intelligence Community Terrorist Threat Advisory" (footnote to *9/11 Commission Report*, p. 255), and on April 13, 2001, the FBI sent a message to all its field offices asking the offices "to task all resources, including human sources and electronic databases, for any information pertaining to 'current operational activities relating to Sunni extremism." The *9/11 Commission Report* points out that this particular memo did not suggest that there was a domestic threat (*9/11 Commission Report*, p. 255), but this has to be taken in the context that, in general, each routine FBI threat advisory presciently pointed out that although threatened attacks were presumed to continue to relate to overseas targets (where virtually every single prior target had been), the FBI "did not rule out a target in the United States" (*9/11 Commission Report*, p. 263).

On September 4, 2001, the military advised the defense and intelligence community's leadership of the value of certain surveillance planes, "perhaps enabling broader air strikes that would go beyond Bin Ladin to attack al Qaeda's training infrastructure" (*9/11 Commission Report*, p. 214). These leaders debated which agency—not merely whether any agency—would be authorized to fire a missile from the surveillance planes, once the technology would be in place for them to be so armed. For the meantime, the head of the CIA directed the continuation of reconnaissance flights. Strikingly, closer to home, on September 10, 2001, the very day before 9/11, Rice's Deputy, Stephen Hadley, gathered various deputies "to finalize their three-phase, multi year plan to pressure and perhaps ultimately topple the Taliban leadership" (*9/11 Commission Report*, p. 214). The events of the following day evidently set in motion the significant acceleration of that timetable.

Virtual illustration of Moore pointing at Bush staring out the window, next to a larger illustration of Bush surrounded by his cabinet members, poring over papers and fixated on the photo of Bin Ladin in the Most Wanted classified ad section.

Topic 25

Did Rice Ignore Clarke's Warnings, or Was It the Other Way Around?

Moore made it seem that had everybody listened to what Richard Clarke had to say, the tragedies of 9/11 could have been avoided. There are only two main problems with this projection. For one, Clarke made the admission referred to above about the limited usefulness of his advice, in terms of averting the tragedies of 9/11. But there is more. Moore went out of his way to make Condoleezza Rice seem disinterested in information about terrorist threats. Yet the 9/11 Commission showed that the dynamics were not necessarily as implied by Moore. At a meeting to discuss al Qaeda May 29, 2001, it was Rice who asked Clarke about "taking the offensive," and it was Clarke who responded "the CIA's ongoing disruption activities were taking the offensive" (*9/11 Commission Report*, p. 204). In other words, Rice was not satisfied, and Clarke felt that the CIA was doing enough, at least in this area, which we now know is universally considered not to have been the case. Rice then asked Clark to go back to the drawing board and outline an ambitious plan of action against al Qaeda. Moore and Clark nevertheless insist that the Bush administration wasn't serious about dealing with al Qaeda prior to 9/11, notwithstanding the evidence referred to in the *9/11 Commission Report* and summarized in this book.

Virtual illustration of Clarke talking to Rice, who paid attention, and then Rice talking to Clarke, who just pointed smugly to his briefcase

Topic 26

Did the Bush Administration Really Cut Funding for Pre-9/11 Counterterrorism?

Contrary to Moore's statement that the Bush Administration cut counterterrorism funding for the FBI (although it did cut some funding within specific programs, especially when prior funded projects hadn't used up the funds allotted from previous years), in terms of total funding the 9/11 Commission reports that the Bush administration decided to propose to Congress a substantial *increase* in counterterrorism funding for national security agencies in its first budget, well before 9/11, including the CIA and the FBI. On 9/11, the FBI was still being run on the Clinton budget, so even had the Bush administration proposed cuts, which it did not, the cuts would not have been in effect on 9/11. In fact, the Bush administration sought an 8% increase in overall FBI funding in its initial budget proposal for fiscal year 2002, including the largest proposed percentage increase in the FBI's counterterrorism program since fiscal year 1997" (*9/11 Commission Report*, p. 209). The Bush administration proposals also included a 27% increase in counterterrorism funding for the CIA (*9/11 Commission Report*, p. 202).

Virtual illustration of President Bush and his supporters putting money into bank-books held by FBI and CIA-types, wearing clothing labelled "Sh!, I'm a secret FBI (or CIA) counterterrorism agent"

Topic 27

How Did the Reaction to Pearl Harbor Compare to the Reaction to 9/11?

The previous pre-9/11 most devastating attack on the United States in this century was at Pearl Harbor, and it was launched by the Japanese. Yet the United States entered the war against the German Nazis, as well, even without having been attacked by Nazis in the middle of the Pacific, let alone in our financial, cultural, and multicultural capital in the largest city in our mainland. Although technically there is a significant difference in that in 1941 the Germans formally declared war on the United States a few days after the Japanese attack on Pearl Harbor, Saddam Hussein declared war on the United States *indirectly* many times prior to the second Iraq war (as discussed in various contexts in this book). It may also be noted that the basic relationship of the United States to Germany prior to World War II had some striking similarities to the relationship of the United States to Iraq prior to Gulf War II to the extent that United States citizens abroad were in mortal danger abroad, in large measure because of the United States' support of its allies—England and France during and prior to World War II or, during and prior to Gulf War II, the Arab Kuwait or the Jewish Israel, though not necessarily on U.S. soil. Similarly, the Germans' declaration of war against the United States essentially threatened United States ships sent in support of its allies, without Germany attacking the United States mainland. Had the United States not declared war on Japan, and not sent any ships across the Atlantic, the Germans might have left us alone, just as Saddam Hussein might have, if we had never defended our allies or our honor or crossed the Atlantic for any other reason. The United States, however, could not be a superpower and an isolationist at one and the same time—in 1941 or in 2001. Somehow mainstream America is not sorry that we fought the Nazis. Yet under Moore's logic in *Fahrenheit 9/11*—and the logic of his comrades-in-putting-down arms—they might have concluded that we should have never fought against the German Nazis or the Italian fascists in World War II.

Moore's indignation that we launched a war against Iraq without having first been attacked may also be seen in the context of the Democratic President Truman's having initiated a war in Korea without having been attacked first; the Democratic President John F. Kennedy's having sent rather aggressive "advisors" against North Vietnam without having been attacked first; the Democratic President Johnson's having escalated that presence into a full-scale war without having been attacked first; and the Democratic President Clinton's having gone to war in Bosnia without having been attacked first.

Virtual illustration of small planes dropping bombs on Pearl Harbor in 1941, with people looking at them with anger and, to the right, larger planes slamming into the World Trade Center, with people looking on in bewilderment.

Topic 28

Pre-9/11 Iraqi Safari for African Uranium and Korean Weapons Systems

As late as in the spring of 2003, Saddam was negotiating with North Korea to buy a missile-production system for weapons of mass destruction (Hitchens, 2004). A few months earlier, President Bush, in his State of the Union address, cited the British for substantiating his allegation that Saddam had sought significant quantities of uranium (obviously for weapons of mass destruction) from Africa. Bush was ridiculed in the press after certain British documents were later found to have been forged, and the CIA backed off its position on the subject. Yet this same press was rather subdued when it came to publicizing the report issued by the U.S. Senate Intelligence Committee early in July of 2004, stating that both the British and French intelligence, as well as other unidentified foreign governments, had notified America of the Iraqi safari for weapons of mass destruction independently (Guggenheim, 2004, Steyn, 2004), and even the British had intelligence from several sources, so if anything, Bush had actually understated his African argument by not referring to the French connection, as well as the reports from other foreign governments. Somehow the CIA's backing off does not carry quite the punch that it would have in the past, considering its record under the leadership of a Clinton appointee, having failed to foresee one cataclysmic event after another, from the first bombing of the World Trade Center to the last, and in between.

Virtual illustration of safari with men in hard hats marching through a jungle toward a big area marked as uranium giving off a radioactive glow.

Topic 29

Did Bush Lie about Weapons of Mass Destruction (WMD)?

The allegation that America went into the war against Saddam in 2003 based on a "lie" that Saddam had weapons of mass destruction has likewise been disproven. First of all, at most, it was based on a mistake, rather than a lie, with the CIA under a Clinton appointee and holdover believing, as did many—if not most—others in high places, and with high-level clearance, as well as many other non-pro-Bush holdovers from the Clinton administration, that weapons of mass destruction were still in Iraq when the war began, in no small measure because if Saddam truly had nothing to hide through and until the point in 1998 when he kicked the weapons inspectors out of his country, then why did he play cat-and-mouse with them so long and so consistently, and why did he want them out of the country in 1998? Had he truly had no weapons of mass destruction in 1998, he should have welcomed their presence and cooperated with them so that they could declare to the world that he had truly eliminated his weapons of mass destruction. When he kicked out these weapons inspectors in 1998, there was virtual unanimity among the nations of the world that he still maintained weapons of mass destruction, and when the war broke out in 2003, he had failed to produce any evidence that many of these weapons of mass destruction had been eliminated, nor had anyone come up with a motivation for destroying them secretly and concealing the evidence of such destruction, knowing that had he destroyed the weapons secretly or otherwise, and had he then provided proof, then even the United States would have had no choice but to advocate the cessation of the search for such weapons, and the discontinuance of economic sanctions and military actions against him.

Findings that Iraq had produced no new weapons of mass destruction between the two Gulf Wars does not mean it didn't harbor such weapons during most of this period, nor does it mean Iraq did not have plans to rebuild its weapons programs of mass destruction after sanctions would terminate, or to buy such systems from other countries, as it was in the process of doing with North Korea, for example (as discussed elsewhere in this book) or to recover such systems which it had sent to other countries for safekeeping (as discussed elsewhere in this book).

Virtual illustration of weapons inspectors knocking on the front door of a big building, while Iraqis are pulling weapons out of the building from the back door, and putting them into trucks

Topic 30

Is It True That No Weapons of Mass Destruction (WMD) Were Found?

A country presents a clear and present danger not merely if its weapons are cocked and ready to be unleashed. Immediately after the war, coalition forces in Iraq found many plans of weapons systems for weapons of mass destruction, as well as "dual use" factories capable of producing massive amounts of weapons of mass destruction. The capabilities were hardly just theoretical. Weapons of mass destruction <u>were</u> reportedly found in Iraq after the war, including sarin, mustard gas, cyanide salt, and live botulinum from which a biological agent can be produced (JINSA Report, June 25, 2004; New York Sun, July 12, 2004), the latter hidden in the home of an Iraqi biological weapons scientist. It is just that the amounts of these weapons of mass destruction were not found in the massive quantities that had been anticipated; however, considering how a few <u>envelopes</u> of anthrax practically stopped the whole vital U.S. postal system for a while shortly after 9/11—as well as all Americans who relied on mail, quantity may not necessarily be as important as the likelihood of use and the likelihood of restoring prior levels of quantity. Furthermore, the 1.77 metric <u>tons</u> of enriched uranium and the 1000 highly radioactive sources found in Iraq after the war (New York Sun, July 12, 2004) are not exactly what would be considered negligible.

Even without finding significant amounts of actual WMD, the troops who searched for them after the major hostilities did find tons of chemical protective equipment, atrophine injectors, decontamination equipment, and chemical warfare manuals all over Iraq (McInerney, 2004), not to mention chemical weapons laboratories (Reuters, 2004), further evidence that the Iraqis were prepared to fight, in the past, and likely to fight again, with considerably more than conventional weapons.

Furthermore, although there was much discussion shortly before the presidential election of 2004 about the Duelfer Report (2004), its finding that there were no weapons of mass destruction in Iraq at the time of the Iraq War of 2003 was offset by a few very significant additional findings—that "Saddam's primary goal from 1991 to 2003 was to have U.N. sanctions lifted," while preserving "Iraq's intellectual capital for WMD"; the Oil-for-Food program (OFF) "could be corrupted to acquire foreign exchange both to further undermine sanctions and to provide the means to enhance dual use infrastructure and potential WMD-related development"; and by 2001 "Iraq was within striking distance of a *de facto* end to the sanctions regime" (Duelfer Report, 2004), so as a practical matter Saddam Hussein was on the verge of rebuilding his WMD programs by 2003, even according to a report cited by Democrats to try to undermine the case that WMD were a valid concern when the United States led the war against Iraq in 2003. Elsewhere we refer to Saddam's efforts to jump-start the process with ready-made weapons systems.

A final thought on the subject, suggested perhaps with tongue in cheek, is that perhaps Saddam Hussein *himself* can be considered a weapon of mass destruction (Giuliani, 2004)!

Virtual illustration of vials of smoking chemicals and barrels of glowing uranium

Topic 31

Did Saddam Smuggle Out WMD Before, During, and After War Began?

It is noteworthy that David Kay, who was in charge of the post-liberation effort to find Iraqi WMD, admitted that even though he and his team failed to find WMD in Iraq, they did find many and well-founded suspicions that people involved in the Iraqi WMD program sold weapons and technical knowledge to anyone with enough money—including terrorists (McInerney, 2004).

Most amazingly, the press seems to have largely covered up, and swept under the rug, the most powerful and sweeping evidence that Saddam did have weapons of mass destruction—thousands of tons of them, immediately prior to, during, and even after the invasion began. It is a miracle of our time that he did not deploy them. Ironically, a primary source for this well-hidden revelation is none other than the United Nations itself (see below)—whose members kept on pressuring the United States not to proceed to war against Saddam on the false grounds that there was no evidence that he had weapons of mass destruction.

Virtual illustration of Saddam Hussein and his soldiers sitting on and hiding weapons of mass destruction as inspectors were expelled from the country

Topic 32

U.N. Personnel Best Witnesses of Iraq's pre-9/11 WMD Smuggling Operation

On June 9, 2004, the United Nations Monitoring, Verification, and Inspection Commission (UNMOVIC) officially briefed the Security Council of the United Nations about the export of Iraqi weapons of mass destruction before, during, and even after the invasion began. According to <u>The World Tribune</u>, the UNMOVIC Acting Executive Chair Demetrius Perricos said that "the Iraqi facilities were dismantled and sent both to Europe and around the Middle East at the rate of about 1,000 tons of metal a month...The Baghdad missile site contained a range of WMD and dual-use components. They included missile components, reactor vessel and fermenters...required for the production of chemical and biological warheads...You can also use it to breed anthrax" (JINSA, June 14, 2004).

Virtual illustration of United Nations officials watching Iraq dismantle weapons of mass destruction, while looking at a calendar stating 2003.

Topic 33

Were any of the WMD Smuggled into Syria?

Geostrategy Direct, an intelligence news service, provides some specifics as to the destination of the weapons of mass destruction that were smuggled out of Iraq shortly before the second Iraq War, referring to "'satellite photographs of Iraqi convoys believed to be bringing missiles and WMD into Syria as well as assertions from Iraqi officials that ousted leader Saddam Hussein ordered such a transfer'" (JINSA Report, January 30, 2004). This is consistent with findings of Israeli intelligence sources right after the war (JINSA Report, January 30, 2004), as well as other sources (Melloan, 2004; McInerney, 2004). Furthermore, just as Americans know exactly where Iraq *used to* hide many of its WMD, Americans now know exactly where Syria *is* reportedly storing its WMD—in no fewer than three specific locations—the first is in a northern Syrian location known as al Baida, in a tunnel complex that the Syrians had originally built for their own WMD. The second location is a Syrian Air Force Camp near Tai Snan. And the third location is in southern Syria, near the Lebanese border, in a city known as Sjinsjam, near the city of Homs (McInerney, 2004). This is not to mention additional locations that have inevitably become repositories of such weapons, hopefully not controlled by "militants," though it is hard to imagine the Syrians not transferring at least some of these weapons to "militants," considering its long record of supporting and arming such people.

It was not in a vacuum that Syrian president Bashar Assad admitted to possessing weapons of mass destruction (McInerney, 2004). So why doesn't the United States make an issue of the transfer of WMD to Syria? One key factor may be that there are no United Nations resolutions on WMD in Syria, as there were on WMD in Iraq (even though the UN failed to follow up some of its resolutions on Iraq's WMD).

Virtual illustration of Iraqis sending trucks of WMD across the border as American soldiers approached

Topic 34

Bottom Line Is That Second Gulf War Led to WMD Disarmament of Two Countries—Iraq and Libya

It would seem that Saddam systematically disarmed and/or placed his WMD in the temporary custody of some of his neighbors and scientists at a time when he needed the weapons the most because he assumed that the U.N. Security Council members he had paid off (as discussed elsewhere in this book) would stop the U.S.-led coalition from carrying out its threat to fight, and even if the U.S.-led coalition would fight, he could weather the war as he did the last time, and then get all or most of his weapons back, and/or begin to rebuild his arsenal without external interference as he had before the first war. The bottom line is that the Gulf War of 2003 clearly was the cause of Iraq's losing its capability to use its weapons of mass destruction, to the extent any were left in his country, or to rebuild its WMD capabilities from scratch, as even many of the war's critics conceded would have been Saddam's plan after sanctions would have been lifted.

Another event not widely anticipated—or at least not widely anticipated so soon—was that Libya's Muammar Gadafi ended his WMD programs abruptly, shortly after the Iraq War of 2003, most likely at least in part because the Libyan leader realized that the United States means business, and he and his country could have been next!

Thus, two rogue countries that were deemed threats to humanity because of their WMD before the 2003 war with Iraq were no longer deemed to be such threats shortly after the war—and the beauty of it is that Libya ended its threat without the United States' having to fire a single shot or lose a single soldier. But it is doubtful that Libya would have laid down its WMD had the United States failed to wage its war with Iraq.

Virtual Illustration of Iraq and Libya, with WMD pulled or dug out of both countries

Topic 35

Did Bush Administration Pressure Military to Exaggerate Danger Posed by Iraq?

Above all, despite all the allegations made by Democrats, Moore, and other morbid accusers of Bush that he and members of his administration pressured the intelligence community to inflate the evidence of pre-war weapons of mass destruction, the bi-partisan Senate Intelligence Committee's report of July 2004 found "no evidence" that the intelligence community's "mischaracterization or exaggeration of the intelligence on Iraq's weapons of mass destruction capabilities was the result of political pressure." Even further, the committee found that intense questioning by members of the Bush administration forced analysts to go back and review their findings, with the result that "The policymakers['] probing questions actually improved the CIA's products" (New York Sun, July 12, 2004).

Virtual illustration showing Bush people asking questions about weapons of mass destruction, and the people giving the answers saying "thank you" for not pressuring us

Topic 36

Two Rebuttals in One,
on WMD and on Iraq-Al Qaeda Links

Allegations that Iraq had no weapons of mass destruction *and* no significant dangerous or operational links with Al Qaeda just prior to the 2003 war against Iraq are also brought into significant question, inadvertently, by leading Bush-basher Clarke. On November 4, 1998, the U.S. Attorney's Office for the Southern District of New York unsealed an indictment of Usama Bin Ladin, the original of which stated, *inter alia*, that al Qaeda had "reached an understanding with the government of Iraq that…on particular projects, specifically including weapons development, al Qaeda would work cooperatively with the Government of Iraq" (*9/11 Commission Report*, p. 128). The language about this understanding was dropped in a superseding indictment filed later that month, but no indication is given by the 9/11 Commission as to why this language was dropped. No less a Bush-basher than Richard Clarke, "who for years had read intelligence reports on Iraqi-Sudanese cooperation on chemical weapons…" speculated "to [Clinton administration National Security Advisor] Berger that a large Iraqi presence at chemical facilities in Khartoum was 'probably a direct result of the Iraq-Al Qaeda agreement.'" Clarke even added that "VX precursor traces found near al Shifa were the 'exact formula used by Iraq'" (*9/11 Commission Report*, p. 128).

Virtual illustration showing Saddam Hussein and Usama Bin Ladin whispering into each other's ears, superimposed on a map of the Middle East, showing the countries of the area, with the two of them standing or seated on Khartoum.

Topic 37

Should Bush Have Gone After Bin Ladin Sooner?

Although Moore seems to imply repeatedly, in the movie, that Saddam Hussein and his heavily-armed "militant" cohorts and allies deserve our empathy and sympathy more than U. S. Republican politicians do, and although he made various claims off-screen that the U.S. was wrong to go to war in Afghanistan without more evidence of the guilt of al Qaeda and the Taliban, Moore nevertheless complains, in the movie, that President Bush waited four weeks before bombing al Qaeda targets in Afghanistan, and two months before launching an all-out war on the heavily-armed "militants" of Afghanistan, implying that the Bush administration purposely was being accommodating to Usama Bin Ladin and his fellow heavily-armed "militants" by giving them a two-month head-start. It should be noted that although heavily-armed "militants" can strike on a moment's notice, wars generally require planning and logistics. Nothing could be more irresponsible than to send soldiers—including many African-Americans, for whom Moore professes special concern and sympathy—into combat without adequate planning and logistical support. The military build-up leading up to the first Gulf War, more than a decade ago, took much more than two months, and the military and political build-up to the second Gulf War against Saddam took, in a way, more than a decade.

Incidentally, to the charge that the U.S. should have sent more than 11,000 troops to Afghanistan immediately after 9/11, it should also be observed that the war against al Qaeda and the Taliban in Afghanistan had broader international support than the war against Saddam, plus an ample supply of home-grown "rebels" (Mauro II, 2004). The U.S. thereby saved many American lives which would otherwise have been lost had President Bush put more in harm's way when other people were willing and able to do the job. Keep in mind that at that time it was still considered very possible, if not likely, that al Qaeda had weapons of mass destruction transmitted to him by the Iraqis or by other "rogue nations," and even though Bin Ladin wasn't captured as of the time this book went to press, the Taliban were still driven from power, and al Qaeda was still driven into its caves.

To put this matter into further perspective, if any president had a perfect opportunity to capture Bin Ladin, it was President Clinton, when Bin Ladin was in the Sudan, and when the government of Sudan was willing and able to turn Bin Ladin over to the United States (Celsius 41.11).

Virtual illustration showing people urging President Bush to hurry up and send the soldiers over to Afghanistan sooner, before they were fully dressed.

Topic 38

Was the "Coalition of the Willing" Constituted of only Exotic Countries?

Moore attempts to belittle the "Coalition of the Willing" by enumerating, with great sarcastic fanfare, the relatively small, exotic, and unsophisticated—let alone unarmed or at most lightly-armed—countries that joined the coalition, such as Palau, Costa Rica, and Iceland.

Moore conveniently leaves out any references to the large and influential countries that did join, such as England, which is not just a country but which is also the head of a 54-country commonwealth of nations (Webster's Dictionary, 2001), and Australia, the latter of which is not merely a country but also an entire continent. Furthermore, the official list of 30 countries of the original coalition of the Gulf War of 2003 (United States Department of State, 2003) omits all Arab countries, including Kuwait, Qatar and Bahrain, which officially provided the United States with bases from which to stage the war, not to mention Saudi Arabia (play on words intended), which is known to have furnished important unofficial support, and the Muslim nation of Pakistan, which is sticking its neck out—as well as making its land and many of its soldiers available—in fighting the war on terror on the Afghanistan front, where its participation is absolutely essential, more essential than the support of virtually any of the members of the coalition in Iraq to that effort, and more essential than virtually any member of the *first* nearly universally appreciated coalition in the *first* Iraq war. The roster of countries in the coalition also omits a reference to Israel, America's closest Middle East ally, which gave it air rights (BBC, 2003) and more enthusiastic support in other ways than many of the countries actually in the coalition. Implying that no large countries joined is in itself most misleading, even if the coalition wasn't quite as large as the coalition during the first Gulf War. Actually, according to the United States Department of State, more countries announced concrete support for the second Gulf War than for the first—and virtually universally admired—Gulf War (BBC, 2003), although this claim has to be taken with a grain of salt, for a variety of reasons, not the least of which are that the members of the original coalition in 1991 may have been more directly militarily involved than some of the members of the present coalition, six of the countries in the present coalition did not exist at the time of the first Gulf war since they were part of the Soviet Union at that time, and an additional two were part of Czechoslovakia at the time of the first Gulf War. The State Department also stated that in addition to the 30 countries officially in the coalition for the second Gulf War, 15 more countries provided assistance, such as intelligence and over-flight rights, but did not want to declare their support officially (BBC, 2003). All of these statistics are a bit curious, considering that U.S. spokesmen during and after the war generally speak of only 30 countries, while a U.S. Senate resolution March 27, 2003 identified no fewer than 50 countries, broken down into three cate-gories—those that actually provided military forces, those that issued declarations finding that Iraq was a threat, and those that provided "diplomatic and strategic support" (Lee, 2004). It should also be noted that some of the people who claim that the Bush administration lied about the relative size of the coalition refer to the numbers of *troops* in the coalition, whereas the Bush administration only claimed that the number of *countries* officially supporting the second Gulf War exceeded the number of countries officially in the first coalition. It has also been estimated, inci-dentally, that the governments supporting the United States in the second Gulf War represent about 1.18 billion people, about one-sixth of the total world population.

It should be noted that even in the nearly universally praised first Gulf War, the coalition was organized more to demonstrate support in principle than on the battle-field. Furthermore, in the present reconstruction of Iraq, which is criticized just about as widely as is the war itself for the supposed lack of participation of other countries, more than half of the countries of NATO are represented with actual soldiers on the ground. In addition, in the supposedly hostile and marginalized United Nations, the most recent four resolutions that were approved in the Security Council on the recon-struction of Iraq prior to an interview with Secretary of State Colin Powell conducted in August of 2004 were proposed by this supposedly discredited and ineffectual coali-tion-builder of the Bush Administration, and passed unanimously (Powell, 2004).

Finally, to those who complain that the United States is sustaining 90% of the casualties in Iraq, it should also be noted that they sustained most of the casualties in the first Iraq war, as well, with one notable difference—now Iraq itself is con-sidered an ally, and now the Iraqi soldiers themselves are sustaining about 40% of the casualties in defense of their own country (Cheney, 2004), and that percentage is likely to grow as time goes on, as the United States' percentage is likely to shrink.

Virtual illustration showing Moore taking attendance of midgets, while Bush is taking attendance of alternating giants and midgets.

Topic 39

Do the Halliburton Contracts Show Favoritism to Republicans or Democrats?

Moore's allegations that the Halliburton company formerly headed by Vice-President Cheney received contracts for rebuilding Iraq without competitive bidding because Cheney was the U.S. vice-president during and after the war are likewise misleading. According to press reports published in response to such allegations, the facts are that Halliburton had what is known as a "requirements contract" with the United States government before the War with Iraq began, and at that time, it won the contract by open bidding, prior to actual need (Mirsky, 2004). This kind of a contract permits the government to require a company to do work based on previously-set costs during periods when going through the usual bidding processes, which can take up to half a year, would be too burdensome to meet an immediate need. Clearly the need for reconstructing Iraq could not wait, and considering the security situation in Iraq, the administration was not necessarily doing Halliburton such a big favor by requiring it to fulfill its contract there! And there is more. This type of a contract with Halliburton not only predated the war, but it also predated the Bush administration, having been signed when the *Clinton* Administration was still in power (Lowry, 2004)! In addition, people familiar with the process have pointed out that because of Halliburton's size and expertise, it was uniquely suited to do the work in Iraq within the necessary time-frame, so that few if any other companies could have really come up with any significant bid in the first place. Furthermore, the General Accounting Office reported that the Army Corps of Engineers was justified in awarding a contract to a Halliburton subsidiary without open bidding because the Defense Department felt that the Halliburton subsidiary was literally the only company that could handle one of its contracts because it had clearance for access to classified information and time was of the essence (Lee, 2004).

Incidentally, some time in 2004, the Halliburton subsidiary won a competitive bid against six other bidders, to continue its oil-related work in Southern Iraq, which means that it probably would have won the earlier uncontested bid even had it been contested.

Virtual illustration showing the signing of a contract by a Halliburton official and a Clinton official.

Topic 40

Are Counterterrorism Programs Over-Funded or Under-Funded?

Moore's complaints that not enough resources are put into counterterrorism, post-9/11, in terms of protecting our borders and the quality of baggage inspectors and supervisors, for example, ring hollow, considering his opposition to President Bush's war on terrorism, to the Patriot Act and other laws enacted to fight this war, and to the money needed to fund the war and maintain the post-war "peace." On the one hand, Moore argues that Bush has created unwarranted fear, and on the other, he ridicules Bush's failure to address these supposedly unwarranted fears, which would arguably infringe on the civil liberties that Moore feels should not be restricted, in deference to the liberties of heavily-armed "militants." Moore ridicules cutbacks in coastline protection, with scenes and testimony about an underfunded Oregon state police, with a bare handful of young men supposedly in charge of the entire coastline—at one point, only one naïve-looking man—and with a telephone that was out of order. What was more seriously out of order was this whole series of scenes. What *Fahrenheit 911* neglects to mention is that the responsibility of protecting the coastline from foreign invaders is not a state function but a federal one. The state police has nothing to do with this function. Rather, it is the responsibility of the United States Coast Guard and the United States Navy. The Coast Guard units assigned to protect the Oregon-Washington State coast consist of over 1000 personnel on active duty, over 450 reserves, and 1600 volunteers (Kopel, 2004).

Virtual illustration showing Moore encouraging Washington to put money into one pocket of homeland security soldier, and taking it out of his other pocket

Topic 41

Does Easier Mean Better, When Describing Dictatorships?

Moore shows Bush stating that a dictatorship would be easier, as if to suggest that this would be Bush's preference, when the context of the statement was that he had just been introduced to the challenges of dealing directly with the leaders of both political parties in Congress (Lee, 2004), so the comment was obviously meant, with tongue in cheek, to suggest that although life may be *simpler* in a dictatorship, it is clearly not *better*—except, of course, for the dictator and his or her cohorts. It should be clear from virtually everything Bush has said on the subject of freedom that he is clearly not an advocate of dictatorship, and to imply otherwise is just another cheap shot at our commander-in-chief.

Virtual illustration showing Moore waving a wand to morph President Bush into Saddam Hussein.

Topic 42

Did Bush Allow Bin Ladin Family to Leave the U.S. Too Soon After 9/11?

The innuendoes that allowing Bin Ladin family members to fly out of the United States immediately after 9/11, even before former President Bush or musical God Ricky Martin were permitted to, seem to illustrate that President Bush allegedly sympathized with Usama Bin Ladin when American officials should have been interviewing Bin Ladin family members. These innuendoes boomerang, however, upon the revelations that, according to the 9/11 Commission, 1) no flights of Saudi nationals took place before the reopening of United States air space on September 13, 2001; 2) the aforementioned Richard Clarke, himself—Bush's then Chief of Counterterrorism, and now one of Bush's current most self-righteous and self-serving tormentors and accusers (and darling of the liberal left)—was the Bush administration official who issued the official approval for the Bin Ladin-laden planes that *did* go out, and no one higher in the chain of command was involved in this decision. Then, contrary to the charges in the film, they were allowed out of the country, only after the FBI had screened the Saudi Bin Ladin passengers, had run their names through federal databases (and the name Bin Ladin should have been no stranger to these databases), had interviewed many of them, had asked many detailed questions, and had satisfied itself that the Bin Ladins who wished to leave this country at that time were of no interest to the United States officials in the search for the heavily-armed "militant" leader in Afghanistan who shared their surname, if not necessarily their personal or political views; 3) the FBI conducted satisfactory screening; no evidence since that time has surfaced indicating that any of the Saudis who left on relatively early flights had links to terrorism (*9/11 Commission Report*, pp. 329—330). To the contrary, most of the Bin Ladin family members living in America had disowned their most famous—and infamous relative (as of 1991 or 1994). Consider the outcries that would have been made by civil libertarians (such as Moore purports to be), had American vigilantes been given opportunities to lynch innocent members of Bin Ladin's family, however distant (in politics as well as geography) they might have been, which would have been most likely had news of their whereabouts in America been revealed (and although they shared Bin Ladin's last name, they did not necessarily share his penchant for murdering civilians or for secrecy).

Virtual illustration showing Bin Ladin Family Members Waiting to be Interviewed by the FBI before boarding planes, with a calendar showing September 13, 2001 in the background.

Topic 43

Is the New Leader of Afghanistan a Double Agent?

The innuendo that Hamid Karzai, the new president of Afghanistan, once served as an advisor to Unocal, one of the main companies Moore linked to President Bush, is introduced by Moore impliedly to question his independence from the pipeline project idea that was aborted long before Karzai came to power. Every moment of the day, Karzai's life is on the line as he builds a society to replace the one dominated by the Taliban and the heavily-armed "militants." To question his integrity to act in the best interests of Afghanistan, as Moore questions Bush's resolve to act in the best interests of the United States of America, brings cynicism to a new level. Even if it were true that Karzai served as an advisor to the company referred to above, he would not necessarily be tainted for life. If everyone who once worked for General Motors, or had family members who worked for General Motors, would have only one point of view, then Michael Moore—who rose to fame based, to a great degree, on his condemnation of that company's leadership in his movie <u>Roger and Me</u>—might still be making home videos in his own backyard, and nothing more.

Incidentally, Unocal issued a statement stating, in part, that "Hamid Karzai, the president of Afghanistan, was never a consultant or adviser to Unocal, as Moore erroneously asserts" (Lee, 2004).

<u>Virtual illustration</u> showing Karzai as a wolf in sheep's clothing, whipping off the clothing the way Superman used to do it, but with a fez hat on his head

Topic 44

Was It So Terrible to Allow Taliban into U.S.A. Before 9/11?

or

Was Bush Really the Best Host the Taliban Had in the U.S.A. Before 9/11?

The innuendo that the Bush administration did something terrible by allowing members of the Taliban into the United States as late as in March of 2001 (allegedly because of Bush's personal interests in a proposed pipeline through Afghanistan advocated by some members of the Taliban but long-since aborted) rings hollow considering what Moore would have undoubtedly said had the Bush Administration *blocked* their entry into the country based purely on the fact that some Taliban leaders may have known where Bin Ladin was hiding half a year prior to 9/11. It is no pipe-dream that Taliban leaders had been negotiating throughout the late 1990s with the <u>Clinton</u> Administration as to such a pipeline, and by the time the Bush Administration came to power, the deal had collapsed. There is, however, evidence that Taliban leaders had offered to review the evidence that the United States had against Bin Ladin, so it was clearly in the interests of the United States for the Taliban leaders to communicate with U. S. officials and in effect negotiate for the possible pre-9/11 turnover of Bin Ladin that could have prevented the calamity of 9/11. Moore implies that President Bush welcomed the Taliban in March of 2001 to improve their image, yet the Bush administration's refusal to recognize their government could not have exactly been the kind of a welcome that could serve any of their possible purposes. Moore also mentioned that the Taliban visited Texas while Bush was governor to discuss the pipeline, but neglected to mention that the Taliban came, at that time, upon being approved by the Clinton administration, and never even met with the then-governor, who had nothing to do with the proposed pipeline, which never materialized. Each time the Taliban came to America after coming to power (at least twice on Clinton's watch, and one on Bush's), the U.S. government stated that the visits did not indicate recognition of the Taliban government and raised concern about the Taliban's record on human rights and its harbouring of Usama bin Ladin (Lee, 2004). The scene in *Fahrenheit 9/11* of a pipeline being built may have been a very well shot scene, of a very well-built pipeline, but it could not have been of a pipeline in Afghanistan, which was never built.

<u>*Virtual illustration*</u> *showing Clinton with more Taliban guests than Bush had.*

Topic 45

Are Minorities Really in the Majority in Combat Positions in the Army?

Moore's innuendo that African-Americans and other minorities are in the majority in the military, and are basically sent to wars to fight and die on behalf of white people because of the poverty of the African-Americans is likewise not supported by statistics, and appears to be designed to foment opposition to the War and to the U. S. efforts to transition to peace and to the stability of the World Order, although the fact that many members of minority groups serve significantly and with distinction is not in dispute, and would not be even if Colin Powell's role would not have been recognized with a rare if not unprecedented promotion to Secretary of State, and even if Condoleezza Rice, President Bush's top National Security Adviser, would not also be an African-American. According to a UPI national correspondent, shortly before the second Gulf War began in 2003 (when the staffing needs of the military for the war were already arranged), minorities constituted about 30% of the general population, and 38 percent of the military, hardly the kind of disparity depicted in the movie. However, some statistics that are of even more interest follow. The enlisted ranks generally came "from neither the top nor the bottom of society," and African-Americans came from households with annual salaries more than $4,000 above the black national average. Ironically, it is the white military population that is poorer than the white national average, by more than $10,000 of family income per year! Furthermore, in arguing against Congressman Rangel's bill to reinstate the draft, the U.S. Defense Department pointed out that African-Americans "have tended to gravitate away from combat jobs." Although African-Americans constituted about 21% of the enlisted force at that time, they constituted only about 15% of combat arms, only about 2% more than their numbers in the civilian population, which means that a higher percentage of whites than blacks in the military are in combat positions! (Sailer, 2003).

   Virtual illustration showing more whites than blacks dying in combat

Topic 46

Does a Truly Enlightened Liberal Force His Children into the Army

Moore's on-camera tongue-in-cheek demands that members of Congress, in their private capacities as individual parents, should commit themselves to enlisting their children into the military, getting them to join, and sending them to Iraq is not exactly a very liberal concept. Minor children are obviously ineligible to join the army, and as to adults, since when do United States citizens—even parents—have a legal right to send any adults anywhere, against their wishes? And even were members of Congress able to do so, as urged by Mr. Moore, most of his liberal supporters would not necessarily feel that the ends in this instance would justify the means, especially if then carried to their logical and consistent conclusions, whereby parents would also be permitted, in Moore's world, to force their adult children to do as their parents please, which would include voting, working, socializing, marrying, praying, preying, smoking (or not smoking), and dressing, based on their parents' deep-seated personal, political, social, religious, and/or idiosyncratic inclinations.

Incidentally, the accusation that George Bush as a young man was supposedly a deserter is overcome by the fact that it is generally uncontested that he received an honourable discharge. Some accusations against him on this subject brought by mainstream liberal newscasters like Dan Rather and others have been exposed as not very honourable, based on outright fraudulent documents.

Virtual illustration showing a member of Congress pointing a gun at his child who is signing a paper at a table next to a soldier.

Incidentally, *Fahrenheit 9/11* portrays a handful of members of Congress being ambushed on screen about this subject, and made them all appear to be stonewalling. In fact, one responded that he had served in the military himself, one responded that he had relatives in the military, and said he would be happy to promote Moore's idea among his colleagues on Capitol Hill, and one was childless (Kopel, 2004). Furthermore, it has been pointed out that most members of Congress' children are not of age for the military (Mauro II, 2004). Also, 101 veterans now serve in the House of Representatives and 36 in the Senate, all of whom have put themselves in harm's way (Kopel, 2004).

It has been noted that although at the start of the war, Senator Tim Johnson was the only member of Congress with a child serving in Iraq, two more members of Congress had sons who were being sent to Iraq in late 2003 or early 2004—Representatives Joe Wilson and Duncan Hunter (Lee, 2004). A researcher working on the premise that only two members of Congress had children serving in Iraq calculated that, believe it or not, these two children represented a higher percentage of the children of members of Congress than the children in the country as a whole are represented in the national average (Kopel, 2004), which makes the statistic about the veterans in Congress all the more amazingly impressive

Much of this information would never have been brought to the public's consciousness, to the extent that it is now, were it not for Michael Moore's attempt to portray our members of Congress in a negative light. Over and above these statistics, the claim has also been made that seven members of Congress (six Republicans and a Democrat) have children in the armed forces (although not necessarily in Iraq): Rep. Marilyn Musgrave, Rep. Ed Schrock, Rep. Joe Wilson, Rep. John Kline, Rep. Tim Johnson, Rep. Duncan Hunter, and Rep. Todd Akin (Rhodes, 2004)

Virtual illustration showing Michael Moore covering a microphone as a militarily decorated member of Congress attempts to speak into it.

Topic 47

Was Moore Digging for Dirt with the Reference to Bush Digging for Bugs?

Not to leave even one stone unturned, we turn now to President Bush's one-sentence statement about digging for bugs, whether or not located under a stone, that makes him appear to be "stoned" himself. It was obviously taken out of context. Anything anybody says can be made to sound off the wall—or under a stone, as the case may be—if taken out of context, and although this writer instinctively laughed along with the rest of the audience, he realizes that what Moore did in this context is so irresponsible that the only emotion a thinking person should come up with is anger that Moore would stoop so low for a laugh at the expense of the leader of the free world. It should be noted, incidentally, that in the society of Saddam Hussein that Moore seems to idealize, toward the beginning of the movie, a bug takes on a far more sinister connotation—that of a hidden microphone. People in Saddam's world would get tortured or killed for the most insignificant statements, if they happened to "bug," in a different sense (to annoy) the then-all-powerful dictator whose regime Moore feels should have been left free to terrorize its own citizens as well as everyone else in the world.

Virtual illustration showing Bush lifting a big stone and showing a big bug with a face like Moore's wearing Moore's traditional baseball cap.

Topic 48

Who in Congress Does Not Read Text of Pending Legislation Before Voting?

The film highlights the complaint that many members of Congress didn't even read the Patriot Act before passing it. What the film passes over, however, is that the law had broad bipartisan support (the Senate bill first passed by a 96-1 vote, and then the vote in the Senate on the final bill was 98-1), members of Congress had adequate time to read early drafts of the bill, even if they didn't have much time to read the final draft (Lee, 2004), revisions are generally marked up in such a way that one does not have to read an entire bill to see the revisions, and any member of Congress who felt more time was needed could have complained to the Congressional leadership before the bill was put to the final vote, and/or could have voted against the bill.

The film shows a member of Congress implying that most of his colleagues in Congress do not read the texts of the bills that they vote into law anyway. What Moore fails to note is that Representative Conyers, the member of Congress he videotaped making this statement, is a liberal Democrat! Although it may be true that many members of Congress do not read the bills they enact into law, and would indeed benefit from an ice-cream truck fitted with a megaphone or loud-speaker cheerfully—or even matter-of-factly—blaring forth the texts of proposed legislation through the streets of Washington, D.C. (as depicted most comically by Moore, with tongue in cheek, and with megaphone or loud-speaker in hand), most of the <u>responsible</u> members of Congress have staff members who read every line, who summarize the main points, who point out the main revisions, and who warn their employers of objectionable clauses buried in the fine print. Moore's decision to place this video clip into his movie, featuring an influential *liberal* who implies that many of his *liberal* colleagues allow the Bush agenda to get enacted because of their incompetence and inattention, seems to show that

101

Moore, as well, not merely fails to read fine print, but did not even seem to have the intelligence and/or the patience to view his own movie carefully, if at all, before approving it for reproduction and distribution—or it could mean that Moore is so far to the left of the political spectrum that he even borrows some precious Bush-bashing time to criticize some liberals as well.

Virtual illustration showing blindfolded lady symbol of justice voting

Topic 49

Did Bush Cut Pay of U.S. Soldiers?
or
Is Bush the REAL Enemy of Our Soldiers?

Moore alleges that the present Bush administration has cut the salaries and benefits of soldiers and has closed Veterans Administration Hospitals. However, according to an official Congressional Research Service Publication, active duty military basic pay has gone up every single year during the past decade, averaging by <u>less</u> than 3% a year during the Clinton years, and by <u>more</u> than 3% a year during the Bush years. (Specifically, the administration request in 1993 was for no increase; the statutory formula was for a 2.2% increase; the 1994 request was for 1.6%, the statutory formula was for 2.6%; the 1995 request was for 2.4%, the formula was for 2.4%; the 1996 request was for 3%, the formula was for 2.3%; the 1997 request was for 2.8%, the formula was for 2.8%; the 1998 request was for 3.6%, the formula was for 3.1%; the 1999 request was for 4.4%, the formula was for 4.8%; the 2000 request was for 3.7%, the formula was for 3.7%; the 2001 request was for between 5 and 10%, the formula was for 4.6%; the 2002 request was for 4.1%, the statutory formula was for 4.1%; the 2003 request was for 4.1%, the formula was for 3.7%; the 2004 request was for 3.5%, the formula was for 3.5% (CRS Issue Brief for Congress, updated July 28, 2004)).

Moore accuses the Bush administration of cutting combat soldiers' pay by 33%, when in fact all the Bush administration had proposed was not to raise the *bonus* for combat pay from $150 to $225 per month (Kopel, 2004). So in fact, the Bush administration was merely not advocating a raise in a bonus, which is a far cry from reducing full salaries (and possibly benefits) by 1/3, as implied by Moore! Actually, the Bush administration ended up not even cutting the bonus by a penny. More significantly, the administration's position on combat pay was quite impressive, when examined in context:

Imminent danger pay was raised for the first time in more than a decade in April of 2003, retroactively, during the Bush administration, after having been left untouched through most of the Clinton years. Furthermore, this raise was set to expire on September 30th, very plausibly because it was obviously intended to benefit the soldiers in the Iraq War, and relatively few politicians expected the soldiers to remain in imminent danger so long after the close of major combat operations. When the issue of the proposed rollbacks hit the front burner, the administration assured the public and its soldiers that it intended "to ensure the [soldiers in combat would] continue to receive...compensation at least at the current levels." Not only has military pay gone up during the Bush administration, but the military has even made progress bridging the pay gap with civilians during this period. In April 2002, the General Accounting Office (GAO) examined the components of the entire military package—including health care, recreational facilities, life insurance, and retirement benefits—and concluded that it was comparable to or in some cases superior to benefits available in the private sector (CRS Issue Brief for Congress, updated July 28, 2004).

Moore accuses President Bush of advocating 60% cuts in assistance to families of soldiers separated geographically by reason of military service, when in fact all Moore was referring to was the administration's *initial* opposition to an increase in an allowance from $100 to $250 (Kopel, 2004). Thus, Moore was consistent only in using the same type of ruse twice to dupe viewers into thinking that the Bush administration advocated a cut rather than simply did not favor as much of a raise as was proposed, at some point, and even *this* opposition was later withdrawn.

Virtual illustration showing President Bush paying soldiers good money in one frame; then, side by side, a civilian line (queue) for services (with wealthy patrons at the front of the line); and a military line for bonuses and services (with combat personnel at the front of the line).

Topic 50

Do You REALLY Think a Wartime Republican President Would Cut Veterans' Benefits?

Moore alleges that the present Bush administration has closed Veterans Administration Hospitals. What he does NOT say is that this administration OPENED veterans' hospitals as well, or that the General Accounting Office concluded in 1999 that the VA at that time spent up to $35 million a year maintaining more than 5 million square feet of vacant space or that the VA was spending billions of dollars operating hundreds of unneeded buildings, or that the VA had multiple facilities in 40 areas (Lee, 2004). As to Veterans' Hospitals closing, this has to be seen in the context of the fact that the proposals to close veterans hospitals were generally directed at hospitals that were located in areas with declining veteran populations, while the Bush administration proposed opening new Veterans' hospitals in areas where the veteran populations were growing. Moore's decision to mention only those that were closing would be as sensible as discussing population figures by only mentioning deaths and omitting references to births. Furthermore, decisions to close veterans hospitals should be seen in the context that it has been estimated that approximately 1100 World War II veterans die every day, at this point. *Of course* this reduces the need for Veterans hospitals.

As to veterans' benefits, President Bush signed the Veterans Benefits Act of 2003 (Public Law 108-183), restoring a variety of benefits, long before Moore's movie accused him of doing essentially the opposite. Some honest misunderstandings on the issue of veterans benefits presumably came about because around the time the second Iraq war began, the House of Representatives passed a resolution which asked House and Senate Appropriations Committee members to reduce the funding of most federal agencies, including the Department of

Veterans Affairs, by 1% in fiscal year 2004; however, even this reduction was proposed in the limited context that (1) it was with the belief it could be made up by cutting waste, fraud, and abuse, (2) it was not targeted specifically at the Veterans Department, but across the board at most agencies; and (3) it never went into effect as to the Department of Veterans Affairs, which ultimately was in fact exempted from the across-the-board budget cuts, thereby demonstrating the importance the Bush administration attached to funding this Department's activities. Furthermore, even had the cuts been applied to the funding of this Department, it would not have cut the Department's budget, in absolute terms—at most it would have simply limited the size of the increase—because President Bush's fiscal year 2004 budget requested a <u>record</u> $63.6 billion for the nation's veterans, including a nearly 8% <u>increase</u> over the fiscal year 2003 budget for discretionary funding, and a 32% increase in overall funding since fiscal year 2001 (Veterans Department News Release, 2003). President Bush consistently proposed increasing the Veterans Affairs department's discretionary budget every year since he took office (Doney, 2004).

Although it is true that President Bush proposed creating a new $250 annual (only once a year) fee for some veterans and more than doubling the agency's monthly drug co-payment to $15, these fees were relatively inconsequential when compared to the major portions of health care, which are subsidized, and these fees were to apply progressively only to veterans who are considered the agency's lowest priority—those who do not have any health care issues related to their military service and who have incomes above certain thresholds (Doney, 2004).

In theory, The official Veterans Affairs position as of the general period of the Iraq War of 2003 was that its only cuts were as to waiting lists for medical care and the backlog of compensation claims—cuts that *favored* veterans (Veterans Department News Release, 2003). As of 2004, for veterans across the board, there was a finding that the <u>backlog</u>—not the numbers—of veterans seeking to have their disability and other health care claims processed by the agency has been cut from a peak of 432,000 to about 331,000; the average wait for those veterans has declined from 233 days to 155 days; and President Bush has added 1,800 claims processors to the VA during the course of his tenure (Doney, 2004).

Virtual illustration of empty hospitals closing, and new ones being built near queues of injured people.

Topic 51

A Look at the Numbers and the Big Picture

Some of the statistics cited above put another very important argument into perspective. As much as we value every human life, 1100 deaths represent the total number of Americans who died in Iraq after about a year and a half after the war began and more than a year after major hostilities ended. World War II, which was fought primarily against an enemy that never attacked our continental homeland, resulted in the deaths of hundreds of thousands of Americans, and millions of Europeans, and Germany did not have the atom bomb when it ended, although it was in a race to develop one when the war began and would have surely developed one within a few years had the United States not entered the war. Does this ring any bells, anyone?

Again, without minimizing the infinite value of every single human life (contrary to the minimizations—let alone tortures—perpetrated routinely in Michael Moore's idyllic Iraq under Saddam Hussein, who should have been left in power, according to Moore), a comparison of additional casualty figures is of interest. No fewer than 1000, but more than 112,000 lives were lost, on the average, in World War II, each year from 1941 to 1945; more than 18,000, on the average, each year from 1950 to 1953 in the Korean conflict, and more than 5,000, on the average, each year from 1965 to 1975, in the Viet-Nam conflict.

Virtual illustration showing World War II deaths compared to Gulf War deaths.

Topic 52

The Infliction of an Unnecessary Layer of Additional Pain

As if Moore couldn't find a single anti-war family burying its dead, he had the outrageous temerity to select unauthorized footage of the burial of a pro-war U.S. soldier in his film—Air Force Major Gregory Stone, described by his family as a "totally conservative Republican" (Kopel). It is as if Moore consciously sought to inflict the soldier's family with an extra totally unnecessary layer of trauma. For a film-maker who claims to be so sensitive, Moore certainly sets a poor example in sensitivity, considering that every decent person, whether pro-war or anti, would have expected him to have at least obtained permission for taking such liberties with the emotions of a family burying its dead—even on the neutral grounds of privacy, let alone the murkier grounds of politics.

When Moore does something that is arguably in poor taste, one has to give him "credit"—he has a tendency to repeat the same type of an action, in one variation or another, so that the reader should not suspect that his questionable action was merely inadvertent. Unfortunately, many people were injured in the war in Iraq and in the efforts to keep the peace afterward, but leave it to Michael Moore to single out one double amputee who did _not_ want to be singled out—at least not in the manner in which he was! Sgt. Peter Damon was portrayed in the movie as feeling disillusioned and abandoned, but he made a point of being interviewed in _Fahrenhype 9/11_ with an upbeat and appreciative attitude that is truly an inspiration. He is looking forward to leading a meaningful life notwithstanding his terrible wounds, and he appreciates what is being done for him in the rehabilitative process. In Michael Moore's defense, it is possible that there aren't many people to choose from who became double amputees willing to speak about their condition on camera. If so, leave it to Michael Moore to find one, so he can be as graphic as he possibly can be in describing the horrors of war, to a world that seems to be relatively oblivious to the horrors of regimes that wage war on their own people, especially if their world view is influenced by films such as *Fahrenheit 9/11*.

Virtual illustration of a soldier shooting with a camera shaped like or morphed into a gun, at a person who is already dead.

Topic 53

Pulling Strings with the Segments That Pull on the Heartstrings

Some viewers feel that the heart of the movie is the saga of Lila Lipscomb, the woman who may receive more camera time in the film than everyone else except possibly President Bush. She is portrayed as an ordinary American whose attitudes were tracked in the movie from a pre-war apparent conservative to an anti-war spokesperson after her son was killed in Iraq. It turns out, however, that she had voted for Bill Clinton and then Al Gore; before the second Iraq War, she was quoted as believing "Bush stole the presidency"; and she has stated she is impressed with Moore's films (Rhoads, 2004). This information would seem to take the heart out of the film's seemingly recurring seemingly persuasive premise that even pre-war conservatives are—and should be—turned off by the decision to fight, the way the war was fought, and the manner in which the peace is being sought. In addition, this information about the pre-war positions of Ms. Lipscomb further calls into question Moore's methodology and credibility.

Virtual illustration showing a person with a liberal logo being motioned to sit on the conservative side of the aisle.

Topic 54

Was What Happened at Abu Ghraib Worse Than *Fahrenheit 9/11*?

Some analysts have contended that the abuses of the prisoners at Abu Ghraib are more damaging to America's reputation than anything Moore may have screened. (For the record, Moore gloats over an implied prison-abuse scene, as well, but it lost its shock value when it was preceded by the Abu Ghraib revelations, as well as the revelation that the victim was not a prisoner—see next entry) The difference between the U.S.' abuses of prisoners, and Moore's arguable abuse of his discretion (to say the least) is that the U.S. has apologized for and repudiated the abuses at Abu Ghraib as having been unauthorized and un-American (but rather based, to an extent, on zealous misinterpretations of imprecise instructions), whereas Moore is far from apologetic about his movie, and what he has done may be considered by many to be not merely un-American, but anti-American.

Incidentally, an independent panel investigating the underlying causes of the prison abuse was chaired by James Schlesinger, a former member of the cabinets of Nixon, Ford, and Carter. The panel found no evidence of a "policy of abuse promulgated by senior officials or military authorities," and found that "no approved procedures called for or allowed the kinds of abuse that in fact occurred" (Lee, 2004).

Virtual illustration of prisoners abused while Americans pull away the abusers, and while Michael Moore and/or his associates and/or photographers smilingly film the abuse (instead of intercepting or disabusing the abusers) while money flows into Moore's camcorder.

Topic 55

Does One Decision by a Commander-in-Chief Render an Entire Army into Childish Pranksters?

Although the American soldiers caught poking fun, in front of Moore's camera, at an apparent Iraqi prisoner of war were clearly abusing their power, Moore's decision to highlight this particular scene in his film only serves to illustrate how Moore was so inept that he repeatedly undermined his own position, even though it was he who controlled his camera. The worst abuse he could find by Americans involves making fun of a drunkard (Kopel, 2004)—not a prisoner of war, since victors do not generally treat their victims with any champagne, let alone with enough liquor to make them drunk. The drunkard was under a blanket, so he was probably too drunk to feel humiliated, and too shielded from view for his identity to be revealed, humiliating his family or himself after he would sober up. What a contrast against Saddam's regime, where the people who abused their power had their fun by routinely and randomly torturing people to death, and what a contrast against today's pro-Saddam "insurgents" in post-Saddam Iraq, who often have their fun by publicly humiliating civilians in front of video cameras, before lopping their heads off, sometimes with a slow dull knife to extend the trauma and the pain. Yet the message Michael Moore attempts to disseminate is, "When a President commits the immoral act of sending otherwise good kids into a war based on a lie, this is what you get." We have explained earlier that the president did not send good kids into a war based on a lie, and even had he done so, no logic could explain how it would necessarily follow that the good kids would act like schoolyard bullies because one political and military decision was made allegedly in error.

Virtual illustration of Americans poking harmless fun at a drunkard, while Saddam tortures people to death, and the post-Saddam insurgents humiliate them before beheading them.

Topic 56

The Ultimate Irony—Pacifist is Causing Bloodshed

On top of everything else, *Fahrenheit 9/11* is now being screened and shown throughout the world, not only by standard commercial distributors, but also, *inter alia*, by terrorist groups, with Moore's consent, if not outright collaboration (*Fahrenhype 9/11*, 2004). Many such groups have never—if ever—permitted their followers to see movies produced in the West before, but made this exception in order to validate their hatred of America, demoralize and alienate our country as well as our allies, pseudo-allies, former allies, and fellow members of the world community of nations, while bringing aid and comfort—and encouragement—to our enemies. Since more U.S. soldiers have died in the line of duty after the cessation of major hostilities and the declaration of military victory in Iraq last year than during the war itself, it is clear that propaganda is stoking the dying embers of the war, re-igniting the fighting, and restoring the post-war fizzle from a simmer to a boiling point at the top of the Fahrenheit level on any thermometer. **The ultimate irony is that Moore's movie in defense of pseudo-pacifism may continue to contribute to the continuing succession of deaths of more Americans after the war than during the war, because it indirectly but inevitably encourages terrorists to keep on fighting, and it encourages would-be—and former—allies to keep on abandoning us in our efforts to get them to share the financial and military burdens of keeping the peace.**

Virtual illustration of light emanating from a movie projector, causing soldiers to die and allies to abandon the United States.

Is this writer alleging that anyone who differs from the president or from the majority view in Congress is un-American? To the contrary, this writer would be the last to condemn and the first to praise honest dissent expressed responsibly. People who write—or film—for foreign as well as domestic consumption have an

117

ethical responsibility to be more careful with what they say than people whose words are unlikely to go very far beyond their own lips or written pages.

Virtual illustration of Moore hitting Bush below the belt.

Topic 57

Another Ultimate Irony: Each DVD Refuting *Fahrenheit 9/11* Outclasses *Fahrenheit 9/11* But Not Reaching Masses

Although at least two DVDs in opposition to *Fahrenheit 9/11* finally became available to the public shortly before Election Day of 2004 (*Fahrenhype 9/11*, 2004, *War, Lies, and Videotape: A Viewer's Guide to Fahrenheit 9/11, 2004*), and a movie even made it to the big screen about two weeks before Election Day (*Celsius 41.11*, 2004), none of these visual rebuttals will come close to being seen by the same numbers of people, for the reasons enumerated in a previous chapter. It is hoped that voters throughout America will see at least one of these visual presentations, to further acquire a balanced perspective, and to see both sides of every major issue addressed in the blatantly one-sided movie, before casting their votes. Let the chips fall where they may, but let them not be tainted or weighted unfairly, let alone hole-punched by voters who may have acted punch drunk. There is an old expression, that "even a cat can spread [the dreaded, highly contagious] cholera [disease]." Unfortunately, even a person with no more talent and knowledge (and, some would say, integrity) than Michael Moore can influence an election, unless his documentary will be put into perspective, on a comparably big screen, for a comparably big audience, in the course of a comparably long period of time. *Fahrenhype 9/11*, in particular, far outclasses *Fahrenheit 9/11* in every respect. Most importantly, instead of being filled with misleading scenes, it fulfils its mission of correcting many of the errors of *Fahrenheit 9/11*. And instead of featuring nameless people rioting and spewing hatred, ill will, and despair, as in *Fahrenheit 9/11*, it features highly intelligent and/or motivated people, such as Dick Morris, Mayor Ed Koch, and Zell Miller, among many others.

Celsius 41.11, which is the movie that rebuts *Fahrenheit 911*, comes across as a true documentary, but that may be its one and only significant drawback. It is cerebral, filled with facts and excellent analysis, and almost completely devoid of entertainment value. Much of what is said in this movie could be said just as appropriately in a political science class in a university, or in a scholarly book review. *Celsius 41.11* may not even have a single talking face recognizable to most Americans, not does it contain a single remark or visual device sure to generate spontaneous applause or even a laugh or a smirk. Ironically, the one rebuttal to *Fahrenheit 9/11* that managed to get into a theatre within a block of Times Square, at the crossroads of the world, before Election Day, is so unexciting that, when this viewer saw it, in prime time on a weekday evening shortly after it was first released, only seven people were in the theatre at the beginning of the show, and only four were left at is conclusion.

Celsius 41.11 goes right after John Kerry, and even cites the leader of the Swift Boat Veterans, but the screen writers are so honorable and decent that they actually have trouble trying to put Kerry in a bad light, no matter how hard they obviously tried! Referring to John Kerry as "the great one," even facetiously, somehow does not quite generate the kind of visceral opposition that Michael Moore had no trouble eliciting against President Bush!

Topic 58

Why Did Moore Suppress What May be Interpreted As Anti-Zionist Views?

Michael Moore has generally not been bashful about his views of the government of Israel and many of its policies. Some of Moore's most famous opinions about Israel are readily apparent from two of his well-known comments that reflect on this Middle East country: "It's all part of the same ball of wax, right? The oil companies, Israel, Halliburton." Also, the dedication of his book, *Dude, Where's My Country?*, was pointedly made in memory of Rachel Corrie, who purportedly died when she climbed onto a bulldozer that was destroying tunnels used by Palestinians to smuggle weapons from Egypt into Gaza, for the purpose of maiming and murdering innocent civilians. Moore's proposed solution to the Middle East problem is also of interest. In his *Dude* book, he suggests giving the Palestinians powerful weapons, and then letting them and the Israelis go at each other head to head, so they could "blow each other up" (God forbid), "and leave the rest of us the hell alone" (Moore, 2003, p. 121–122).

Even if Moore is saying the truth when he says he does not oppose the Jews per se, an argument can be made by some people that the last quotation just cited would make him a true anti-Semite in addition to being a true anti-Zionist, since Arabs and Jews are both traditionally considered descendants of the Biblical Shem, in whose name the term anti-Semite is rooted. By rooting against Arabs as well as Jews in this instance, some people might deduce that Moore reveals something rather telling about his level—or dearth—of idealism and compassion. "A pox on both of your houses," might be his sophisticated and principled way to stop the pain, suffering, and humiliation that so many Arabs and Israelis have been suffering for generations.

Not only does the above position expose him to accusations by some people that he is a true anti-Semite, but also to accusations by some people that he is even more of an anti-Semite than most anti-Semites, since most people who are considered anti-Semites focus their hatred only on the Jews, while Moore does more—he apparently would like to see millions of innocent Palestinians die as well, if he is to be taken at his word in this instance, and not just a natural death, but death by military means, which could be particularly painful and agonizing.

The conspicuous absence of Israel from *Fahrenheit 9/11* has been noted by others (e.g., Troxler, 2004). Even some non-anti-Semites—or at least SUBTLE anti-Semites—believe that the United States did not enter the war in order to eliminate the threat of weapons of mass destruction from a dictator likely to at least transfer some to terrorists (were he not to use them himself against America, as he used them against his own people) or likely to renew or develop WMD programs after the sanctions would be lifted, nor do they believe that President Bush took this country into war to eliminate the possibility that Saddam Hussein would at some point reduce or eliminate the flow of Middle East oil to this country (or even just to world markets), with or without gaining control of Kuwait again, or Saudi Arabia, whether or not he would use the threat of weapons of mass destruction and/or blackmail. Many people simply believe that President Bush led the United States into war to satisfy a few "neoconservatives" who happen to be Jews (and thereby upset, incidentally, some "pure" conservatives).

One answer given to explain the omission of any reference to Israel in *Fahrenheit 9/11* is that the movie was designed primarily to convince and energize people to vote against President Bush (Troxler, 2004), and the majority of Jews traditionally vote for the Democratic candidate for President no matter how much more philo-Semitic the Republican candidate may be. It has been speculated that Moore didn't want to turn off Jewish voters.

The Jews often serve the interests of politicians in various ways: (1) they often vote in blocks, especially the ultra-Orthodox, who in some instances follow their rabbis' personal as well as religious views; (2) they are disproportionately represented in "swing" states, (3) they are represented in the media and in the world of comedy disproportionately, and above all, (4) they donate a disproportionate amount of their money to charities in general, and political candidates, as well. There is good reason to believe that Moore didn't want to alienate them.

Jews and Zionists are also represented disproportionately in many of the arts, including not just film-making, but also film distribution. Mr. Moore did not become a multimillionaire for nothing. There is every reason to believe that he could have anticipated that, somewhere down the line, he might have some trouble distributing *Fahrenheit 9/11* due to its obvious political slant, and due to the manner in which he conveyed it. Antagonizing Jews and Zionists might not be helpful. As it turns out, Disney decided not to distribute *Fahrenheit 9/11*, and Moore ended up having it distributed with substantial backing from at least one prominent Jewish source.

Virtual illustration of a roll of film with a blank spot in the middle shaped like the country of Israel.

Topic 59

Some Observations about Style

Although the focus of this critique has been on the *substance* of *Fahrenheit 9/11*, no analysis of the film would be complete without a reference to Michael Moore's cinematic techniques. The movie is truly a multi-media production. Although most true documentaries let the historic events speak for themselves, in the presence of a camera or camcorder, Moore's "documentary" stands out for its ability to portray people attempting to advance a particular point of view, and presenting their words in such a way that they have the opposite effect—from President Bush himself, right on down to many members of his staff, including Secretary of State Colin Powell, National Security Adviser Condoleezza Rice, and Attorney General John Ashcroft. All are shown attempting to defend the war in Iraq, in one way or another, but their words or deeds are portrayed in a counterproductive manner.

It might be fair to say that this "documentary" is an appeal not primarily to the intellect of its viewers, but also, through its biting sarcasm and wit, to the jugular vein and the funny bone, not to mention the heartstrings as well. Rather than focusing on the subject, the camera, and the chronological sequence of events, this true multi-media production focuses just as strongly on the scissor (to splice segments out of context), on the pen (to insert very opinionated commentary), on the eraser (to omit key information, such as about Saddam Hussein's record of torture and murder), on the musical instrument (setting up scenes by intentionally advancing Moore's anti-Bush agenda by using cheerful or frivolous music when solemnity or seriousness would be appropriate, and solemn music when inspirational or optimistic music would be appropriate), and, above all, on the imagination (to instill thoughts into the viewer that would never come to mind were the film to focus on the hard facts in context).

Virtual illustration of Moore with a camcorder, but with a background of a man with a pen in one hand and a scissor in the other hand, and an orchestra in the background.

Topic 60

Psychological Arguments Regarding the film as an Instrument of Propaganda

Many who have analyzed *Fahrenheit 9/11* have described it as more of a propaganda piece than as a documentary. Dr. Kelton Rhoads, an adjunct professor at the University of Southern California, who has been described as one of America's leading authorities on the use of psychology and propaganda in modern culture, has written a brilliant and comprehensive analysis of the film (Rhoads, 2004), in terms of how it utilizes eleven basic features of classic propaganda. It is available on the Internet, and four of its features appear in condensed form in Troxler, 2004.

Rhoads places most of the weaknesses of the film into the following 11 features of classic propaganda (the examples in parentheses are not in Rhoads' words)

- Omissions (e.g., no references to Saddam's mass tortures and mass murders),
- Contextualization (e.g., pointing out the dangers of flying, but recommending that we fly anyway),
- Ingroup/Outgroup Manipulations (e.g., targeting Saudi royal family as outgroup, blurring the line with the anti-government Bin Ladin Saudi terrorists; with the Bushes in the ingroup).
- Cynicism (impute negative motives, like fighting Iraq to keep Americans in fear)
- Traps (catch 22's: e.g, if terror strikes, Bush didn't do enough; if it doesn't strike, he did too much),
- Manipulating Cause and Effect (Bush "responsible" for 9/11, notwithstanding the co-culprits enumerated in the *9/11 Commission Report*; Bush "responsible" for the abuse of prisoners, not because Moore abused facts, but because, in Moore's world, Bush brought the country to war "based on a lie")

- Modeling the Convert Communicator (focusing on people who apparently switched positions, but in the case of the movie's leading lady, who did *not* necessarily do so, as described above)
- Pacing and Distraction (e.g., showing facts and headlines too quickly to be processed, when a careful reading would expose the misleading nature of their use)
- Associations (e.g., linking Bush with Taliban because of unrelated Texas visit approved by then-incumbent President Clinton)
- Numeric Deceptions (e.g., Saudis' slice of America no cause for indigestion, compared to Moore's figures), and
- Shutting Down the Opposition (pre-emptively threatening to sue anyone who will libel him)

  All who may still question the characterization of the film as propaganda should consider whether they knew, when watching the film, that Michael Moore is on record, elsewhere, as having stated that "There is no terrorist threat in this country. This is a lie. This is the biggest lie we've been told" (Slevin, 2003); (2) whether they were aware of this position of Michael Moore when seeing his movie; (3) whether they agree with it; and (4) whether they feel Michael Moore was honest with them in writing and producing the movie as he did, if this was his belief in 2003.

Virtual illustration of Michael Moore lying on a couch, and breaking it

Topics 61–83

Additional Topics

For additional relevant information, the writer recommends all the material in the References that appear below, especially as documented on the Internet website of Dave Kopel (2004), which elaborates on many of the points referred to above, and which provides annotated responses by Moore, to the extent Moore felt he had anything to say in his defense. Kopel's unabridged piece is available on the Internet as cited below, and in condensed form in Troxler, 2004. The following points documented by Kopel supplement those that appear above, and are hereby summarized and/or elaborated on as follows:

Topic 61—Purported Post-Election Victory Party Was Only a Pre-Election Rally

The movie began with a rally that was portrayed as a victory celebration by the supporters of Al Gore for president. This scene was used for the purpose of setting the stage for the dramatic accusation that the Bush supporters stole the election. Actually, the rally was merely a pre-election event, but presenting the truth would not have been as dramatic. Whether this set the stage for the movie in general or for a pattern of deception as well is an issue everyone exposed to both sides of every topic described in this book is welcome and encouraged to decide.

Topic 62—Role of Katherine Harris

Florida Secretary of State Katherine Harris was not Florida's "vote count woman," as alleged by Moore; the election commissioners in each of Florida's counties were authorized to and did count the votes; the Secretary of State merely certifies the vote.

Topic 63—*The Only Way Gore Could Have Won*

Jeffrey Toobin, a lawyer cited by Moore, admitted on CNN—in a segment not shown by Moore—that the only way Gore could have been declared the winner in Florida would have required a type of recount that even Gore had never even proposed in any of his lawsuits and which would have not been permitted under Florida law, anyway.

Topic 64—*Florida Election Result "Article" Was Really Only a Letter*

An "article" purportedly in *The Pantograph*, in Illinois, purportedly claiming that the "Latest Florida Recount Shows Gore Won Election," was actually only a letter to the editor.

Topic 65—*The Inauguration Day Protests Did Not Stop Bush From Getting Out of His Car*

Moore claimed that the protests on the inauguration day prevented Bush from getting out of his limousine to walk part of the way to the White House. The BBC reported, however, that "Bush delighted his supporters by getting out of his limousine and walked the last block of the parade, holding hands with his wife, Laura."

Topic 66—*There HAD Been Comparable Inauguration Day Protests*

Moore claimed that there had been no comparable protest to an inauguration. In fact, anti-Bush organizers expected 20,000 protesters to show up, while the anti-Nixon protest in 1973 featured 60,000 people.

Topic 67—*The First 8 Months of the Bush Presidency*

Moore alleges that during the first 8 months of the Bush presidency, things got no better for Bush than the riot that took place on inauguration day, and Bush had trouble getting legislation passed. In fact, Congress enacted the top item on Bush's legislative agenda, the tax cut, and the House of Representatives easily passed the "No Child Left Behind" education bill, entitled H. R. 1, showing its importance to the administration. After 9/11, this bill was passed in the Senate, and enacted in the law, as were many others.

Bush also barely dipped in the polls during his first 8 months in office.

Topic 68—Bush Was Not Considered a "Lame Duck" president in 2001

No serious commentator referred to President Bush as looking like a "lame duck president" in September of 2001.

Topic 69—Gore Addressed the Same "Base" as Bush, at a Charity Event

Bush's reference to wealthy participants at a formal dinner as his "base" was said in jest. In context, Al Gore addressed the very same audience at the very same dinner; Gore also made self-deprecating jokes at the dinner, and the purpose of the dinner was to raise money for poor people.

Topic 70—Bush Didn't Spend the Last Week at His Ranch, Nor Was he in Florida

Fahrenheit 9/11 states that Bush spent the last week of August 2001 at his ranch, which is contradicted by a schedule including appearances in, *inter alia*, Pittsburgh, Williamsport, San Antonio, Waco, and Washington, D.C., but not Florida, where Moore claims Bush *did* go to at the end of his vacation!

Topic 71—The Book Bush Picked Up on 9/11 Was NOT Entitled "My Pet Goat"

Moore claims that the book Bush picked up at the elementary school on 9/11 was called "My Pet Goat." In fact, it was entitled "Reading Mastery 2," and merely contained an exercise entitled "The Pet Goat." Even the exercise was not called "My Pet Goat."

Topic 72—Moore Himself Wanted to Fly When He Said Nobody Did

Ironically, although Moore states in his movie that nobody wanted to fly on September 13, 2001 except the bin Ladins, in fact Michael Moore wrote to his fans at that time that he himself wanted to fly home from where he was stranded, on 9/11.

Topic 73—At Most, the Saudis Own 7% of Foreign Investments in America, Not 7% of America.

Topic 74—President Bush Cooperated with the 9/11 Commission; 2 Agencies Didn't

Although it is true that the 9/11 Chair Kean raised Cain about inadequate cooperation by the administration, he was referring to two agencies—Justice and Defense—not the White House. Eventually, Kean praised the Bush administration for giving his Commission "unprecedented access to relevant records."

Topic 75—John Ashcroft Did Not Lose to a Dead Man

John Ashcroft did not lose to a dead man, as alleged in the movie. After his opponent for the Senate seat in Missouri passed away during the campaign, the Democratic governor informed the voters of that state that a vote for Ashcroft's opponent would result in the appointment of the recipient of the sympathy vote for the decedent's widow.

Topic 76—The Chair of the House Committee on Intelligence HAD a Toll-Free Number

The Chair of the House Permanent Select Committee on Intelligence did not indeed have an 800 number for Patriot Act complaints, but he did have a toll-free number, which the film failed to disclose.

Topic 77—Bush Was Correct as to When Major Combat Operations Ended

Although President Bush did indeed declare that "major combat operations in Iraq have ended," he was not incorrect in saying so, as implied by Moore; Bush <u>also</u> said at the same time that our coalition is still very much engaged in dangerous work securing and reconstructing the country.

Topic 78—The American Press Wasn't Universally Naively Biased in Favor of the Iraq War

Moore portrays the American press as naively biased in favor of the Iraq war, but even this portrayal is misleading since, in fact, there is no evidence in the film that the American press was naïve or biased in favor of the war; to the contrary, some major anchors were actually critical of the war. The scene of Peter Jennings stating that Saddam's army had collapsed in April 2003 does not reflect any naive bias on his part, just the simple truth.

Topic 79—Ms. Lipscomb's Son Apologized; His Widow Had No Need to

Moore failed to disclose that Ms. Lipscomb's son apologized for a critical letter he wrote about the war, and his separated widow does not share even his temporary expression of hatred.

Topic 80—Equal Time to Bereaved Families Who Supported the War

The movie fails to give equal time—or any time—to the feelings of bereaved families who supported the war, although it didn't hesitate to invade their privacy against their will, as indicated above.

Topic 81—Enron Never Stood to Profit from the Afghanistan Pipeline That Was Never Built.

Topic 82—Bush Sold Stock Only After Checking with Lawyers

Bush sold stock only after checking with the lawyers at Harken Energy who had at one point warned its directors not to do so under certain circumstance.

Topic 83—Moore Praises and Encourages the Enemy

On camera, Moore purports to support our troops. Off camera, he has stated that the Iraqis who have been fighting against the Americans and the new Iraqi government are not corrupt or enemies, but "the revolution, the minutemen, and their numbers will grow, and they will win."

References

AFP, "French Anger at Duelfer Report Charges over Iraq Corruption," Washington, October 7, 2004.

Agnes, Michael (editor in chief), Webster's New World College Dictionary, 2001.

BBC News World Edition, Internet, March 18, 2003, citing, *inter alia*, the United States Department of State.

"Bush's Intelligence," *New York Sun*, July 12, 2004, p. 8.

Celsius 41.11, movie directed by Kevin Knoblock and released by Citizens United, beginning October 20, 2004.

Cheney, Dick, Vice-Presidential Debate, October 5, 2004

Diney, Jim, "Kerry Decries Budget Cuts by Bush, But There Have Been None in the Usual Sense," http://www.tblog.com/templates/index.php?bid=jimdoney&static=157857, April 23, 2004.

Duelfer, Charles, Comprehensive Report of the Special Advisor to the Director of Central Intelligence on Iraq's Weapons of Mass Destruction, September 30, 2004 (but released to the public on October 7, 2004).

Ethics and Public Policy Center, War, Lies, and Videotape: A Viewer's Guide to Fahrenheit 9/11 (in DVD and on the Internet at EPPC.org).

Fahrenheit Facts Blog, http://fahrenheit fact.blogspot.com

"Florida Ballots Project—In-Depth Special," CNN.com. http://www.cnn.com/SPECIALS/2001/florida.ballots/stories/main.html.

Gingrich, Newt, Interview on Fox News Sunday, August 1, 2004.

Giuliani, Rudolph, in a speech at the Republican National Convention in New York City, August 30, 2004.

Goldich, Robert L., "Military Pay and Benefits: Key Questions and Answers," Congressional Research Service (CRS) Issue Brief for Congress, updated July 28, 2004.

Guggenheim, Ken (of the Associated Press), "Iraq Uranium Claim Gets Some Support," http://aolsvc.news.aol.com/news/article.adp?id=20040718121809990005, July 18, 2004.

Hayes, Stephen S., *The Connection: How al Qaeda's Collaboration with Saddam Hussein Has Endangered America*, New York: HarperCollins, 2004.

Hays, Jeff (executive producer), Dave Sapp, Mike Fox, and Steve Haugen (producers); Peterson, Alan, director, *Fahrenhype 9/11*, http://www.fahrenhype911.com, October 5, 2004.

Hitchens, Christopher (columnist for *Vanity Fair*), "Unfairenheit 9/11—The Lies of Michael Moore," msn, http://slate.msn.com/id/2102723/., June 21, 2004.

Isikoff, Michael, and Hosenball, Mark, "More Distortions from Michael Moore— Some of the Main Points in 'Fahrenheit 9/11' Really Aren't Very Fair At All, *Newsweek* Internet http://www.msnbc.msn.com/id/5335853/site/newsweek/, June 7, 2004.

Kean, Thomas H., et al., *The 9/11 Commission Report*, New York: Government Printing Office and W. W. Norton & Company, 2004.

Konner, Joan, Risser, James, & Wattenberg, Ben, "Television's Performance on Election Night 2000: A Report for CNN, Jan. 29, 2001.

Kopel, Dave, "Fifty-Nine Deceits in Fahrenheit 9/11," Independence Institute, Denver, Colorado. www.davekopel.org. The condensed version is reproduced in Troxler, 2004.

Lee, Stephen, *FootnoteFahrenheit* (Internet site), 2004.

Lott, John, & Blase, Brian (of the American Enterprise Institute), "Moore's Myths— Fairytales of 'Fahrenheit 9/11", *The New York Post*, July 13, 2004, p. 2.

Lowry, Rich, "Dump Cheney?", *The New York Post*, July 16, 2004, p. 29.

Mason, Linda, Francovic, Kathleen, & Jamieson, Kathleen Hall, "CBS News Coverage of Election Night 2000: Investigation, Analysis, and Recommendations," Jan. 2001.

Mauro, Ryan, Responding to Michael Moore, Moorelies.com.

Mauro, Ryan (Mauro II), Response to Michael Moore, Part Two, Moorelies.com.

McInerney, Lt. General Thomas, and Vallely, Maj. General Paul, *Endgame—The Blueprint for Victory in the War on Terror*. Washington, D.C.: Regnery, 2004.

Melloan, George, "Some Recent Victories in the War on Terror," *Wall Street Journal,* August 24, 2004, p. A13.

Mirsky, Stuart, "Response to an Angry Bush-Basher," *The Jewish Press,* July 2, 2004, p. 2.

Moore, Michael, "*Fahrenheit 9/11,*" Lion's Gate, 2004.

Moore, Michael, Interview in serious interview segment of The Tonight Show, NBC, July 30, 2004, between 12:00 o' clock midnight and 12:30 A.M.

Mylroie, Laurie, *The War Against America: Saddam Hussein and the World Trade Center Attacks: A Study of Revenge* (New York: HarperCollins, 2001).

"News Release—Principi Decries Myth of Budget 'Slash,'" Department of Veterans Affairs, April 24, 2003.

Powell, Colin, interview, "Special Report with Brit Hume," Fox News, August 5, 2004.

Public Law 108-183, Veterans Benefits Act of 2003.

Reuters, "Chemical Weapons Lab Found in Falluja—Iraq Minister," Netscape News, retrieved over the Internet November 25, 2004

Rhoads, Kelton, Propaganda and Fahrenheit, www.workingpsychology.com/fahrenheit.html; the first four features are excerpted in Troxler, 2004.

Sailer, Steve, "Are Soldiers Black and Poor?" United Press International, Washington Politics & Policy Desk, January 16, 2003.

Sayfie, Justin, www.centigrade9ll.com

Slevin, Niamh, "Moore Discusses Book, Blasts 'Bush of Arabia,'" The Michigan Daily, October 13, 2003)

Steyn, Mark, "A Movement in Denial," The Sun, July 12, 2004, p. 8.

"Summer Weekend Roundup," Jewish Institute for National Security Affairs (JINSA) Report No. 420, June 25, 2004, p. 1.

Troxler, Lee, *Fahrenhype 9/11—Companion Book—Unravelling the Truth about Michael Moore's Fahrenheit 9/11.* www.fahrenHYPE911.com (2004)

Unger, Craig, *House of Bush, House of Saud: The Secret Relationship between the World's Two Most Powerful Dynasties.* New York: Simon & Schuster, 2004.

"UNMOVIC Comes Clean on Saddam's WMD and It's Worried," JINSA Report No. 416, June 14, 2004.

Williams, Stephen, *How to Be a President*. San Francisco: Chronicle, 2004.

"Whoa There," JINSA Report No. 387, January 30, 2004.

Acknowledgments

I hereby acknowledge, with appreciation, all of the authors whose works are referred to in this book, for doing so much, each in his or her own way, to call attention to the ways in which *Fahrenheit 9/11* can and should be rebutted. Their names are all identified in the Reference Section, and most of the primary ones are identified in the Sources section, as well. I found every point to be fascinating and helpful in further documenting and supplementing my own findings and analysis.

My thanks are also extended to Sergey Sokoloff, the artist who drew a most comprehensive caricature specifically for the cover of this book

I appreciate the time and energy spent by three people, in particular, who sought to convince various mainstream publishers to produce this volume, knowing that most publishers require a lead time of more than half a year for the publication of a book, and my manuscript wasn't ready to submit to a publisher until about two months before Election Day, the ideal time by which this book should have been read by readers for maximum effect (although this book should also be of particular interest until the Academy Awards will be issued, considering that *Fahrenheit 9/11* is likely to remain in the spotlight at least until that point in time, and beyond). In deference to the privacy of these three individuals, and considering that they did not succeed, nor did anyone else, to my knowledge, in having a book on this topic published by a mainstream publisher before Election Day, I will not name these three individuals, but I will note that one is a radio personality who is a household name, one is a Nobel-prize winner who is a household name, and one is an international literary agent who undoubtedly will help make many people into household names in the course of her career, even if she will choose to continue to remain behind the scenes in her present role.

I express my appreciation to my colleagues at the law firm at which I work, including those who disagree with my views, for providing me with insights and leads nevertheless, and for tolerating my obsession to defy the odds and get this book published before Election Day, 2004, one way or another, which mission was accomplished with a limited First Edition. In deference to some of the firm's clients whose views may be different from mine, I will protect the firm's privacy to the extent these clients and people close to them do not know my identity and/or do not find out about this book.

I am pleased to acknowledge, with deep appreciation and admiration, Isabella, my charming wife, her constructive criticisms, and her consistent encouragement. I also appreciate the encouragement and the mature understanding of my dear children, Raphael and Ariella, beyond their tender years.

Above all, I am grateful that I still have a positive and appreciative outlook on life. In the context of this book, perhaps I even owe some measure of appreciation to two most unlikely sources—(1) Michael Moore, for unwittingly presenting me with such an interesting intellectual challenge, and for giving me some positive things to say about his film (however few and far between they may be), and (2) the mainstream publishers that did not accept my manuscript (because they could not get it into their lists and catalogues in time to be most meaningful), since their refusal resulted in a) my continuing to attempt to improve it and expand on it so that it is far more accurate and complete than it was when I first submitted it, and resulted in b) my getting a first edition into print before Election Day, which made it potentially more meaningful than it would have been had it first been published four or more months later.

Notwithstanding the fact that a traditional mainstream publisher has not decided to publish this book at this point, I appreciate the publisher that DID accept my manuscript; I appreciate what it has done to enhance my manuscript; I appreciate what it pledges to do in the future with my book; and I appreciate its role as a leader of the publishing industry of its genre, and probably the one that is generally most highly recommended and respected.

Index

NOTE: Index entries are identified by Topic number. Topics appear in numerical order. In most instances involving the main (first) 60 topics, a new topic begins on every odd-numbered page. In some exceptional cases, new topic numbers will appear on the odd-numbered page immediately *following* the next odd-numbered page.

0-595-33740-6